NOTHING BUT THE TRUTH

with Connections

ALSO BY THE AUTHOR

Windcatcher

The True Confessions of Charlotte Doyle

The Man Who Was Poe

Something Upstairs

Romeo and Juliet—Together (and Alive!) at Last

Wolf Rider

Bright Shadow

S.O.R. Losers

Devil's Race

The Fighting Ground

Shadrach's Crossing

Sometimes I Think I Hear My Name

Who Stole the Wizard of Oz?

A Place Called Ugly

The History of Helpless Harry

Man from the Sky

Encounter at Easton

Night Journeys

Emily Upham's Revenge

Captain Grey

No More Magic

Snail Tale

Things That Sometimes Happen

NOTHING BUT THE TRUTH

a documentary novel

by AVI

with Connections

HOLT, RINEHART AND WINSTON
Harcourt Brace & Company

Austin • New York • Orlando • Atlanta • San Francisco
Boston • Dallas • Toronto • London

For permission to reprint copyrighted material, grateful acknowledgment is made to the following sources:

Orchard Books, New York: *Nothing but the Truth* by Avi. Copyright © 1991 by Avi. Jacket illustration © 1991 by Peter Catalanotto. All rights reserved.

Avon Books, Inc.: Prolog, Scene One, and Scene Two from *Nothing But the Truth: A Play* by Ronn Smith, based on the novel by Avi. Copyright © 1997 by Ronn Smith. **Free Spirit Publishing, Inc., Minneapolis, MN (800) 735-7323:** "Character in ACTION, Jana Benally: Telling the Truth" (retitled "The Courage of Jana Benally") from *What Do You Stand For? A Kid's Guide to Building Character* by Barbara A. Lewis, edited by Pamela Espeland. Copyright © 1998 by Barbara A. Lewis. All rights reserved. **Anna Guest:** "Beauty Is Truth" by Anna Guest from *Stories from Seventeen*. **HarperCollins Publishers:** "Mr. Entwhistle" and "Today" from *Hey World, Here I Am!* by Jean Little. Copyright © 1986 by Jean Little. **Little Simon, an imprint of Simon & Schuster Children's Publishing Division:** From "The Star-Spangled Banner" from *The American Flag* by Thomas Parrish. Copyright © 1973 by Cord Communications Corporation. **Random House, Inc.:** From "Making News" from *Living Out Loud* by Anna Quindlen. Copyright © 1988 by Anna Quindlen.

Cover photos: Andrew Yates

HRW is a registered trademark licensed to Holt, Rinehart and Winston.

Printed in the United States of America
ISBN 0-03-054666-4

17 18 19 20   043   09 08 07

Contents

FOR BETTY MILES

Two Questions

Do you swear to tell the truth,
the whole truth, and
nothing but the truth?

Does anyone say no?

MEMO

HARRISON SCHOOL DISTRICT

Where Our Children Are Educated, Not Just Taught

Dr. Albert Seymour
Superintendent

Mrs. Gloria Harland
Chairman, School Board

STANDARD FORMAT FOR
MORNING ANNOUNCEMENTS ON
PUBLIC-ADDRESS SYSTEM

1. 8:05 A.M.   The Principal, or in his stead the Assistant Principal, or in his stead a designated member of the faculty, will say, "Good morning to all students, faculty, and staff. Today is Monday (or whatever day), January (or whatever month) 3 (or whatever day). Today will be a Schedule A (or B) day" (depending on what schedule).

2. Say, "Today in history . . ." (Please consult *Book of Days* in Principal's office for appropriate references. Limit is three items.)

3. Say, "Please all rise and stand at respectful, silent attention for the playing of our national anthem."

4. Turn on tape of anthem.

5. After anthem is complete, say, "I have these announcements." All administration and faculty announcements shall be made at this point.

6. Say, "May I now introduce _____ (name of stu-

dent, grade) for today's sport and club news. Have a good day."

7. Student announcements.

8. All announcements should end by 8:15 latest.

DR. JOSEPH PALLENI
Assistant Principal

1

Tuesday, March 13

10:35 P.M.

From the Diary of Philip Malloy

Coach Jamison saw me in the hall and said he wanted to make sure I'm trying out for the track team!!!! Said my middle school gym teacher told him I was really good!!!! Then he said that with me on the Harrison High team we have a real shot at being county champs. Fantastic!!!!!! He wouldn't say that unless he meant it. Have to ask folks about helping me get new shoes. Newspaper route won't do it all. But Dad was so excited when I told him what Coach said that I'm sure he'll help.

Saw a thing on TV about Olympic committees already organizing all over the country. Olympics. I'm going to be there! County champs. State champs. College champs. Then Olympics! Folks always reminding me about the money they're putting aside for my college, which is the only way to go. That's what did Dad in, dropping out. Too hard to get noticed with just clubs.

Rainy and cold. I hate this kind of weather. Slows you down. Still ran six miles. I'm getting stronger.

Oh, yeah. . . . At lunch Sarah Gloss came up and said she had to speak to me. Said this girl, Allison Doresett, likes me. I had to act cool because I wasn't sure who she was. Then I remembered she's in my English class and is really decent. She must have liked that gag question I asked. The two of us would be front-of-the-line. Bet she heard about my running too. Girls go for guys who win. Ta-da! It's Malloy Magic time!

Talk about Malloy Magic. . . . This time for—da-dum!— Miss Narwin. I mean, what can you do with an English teacher who's so uptight she must have been put together with super glue. Try to make a joke—lighten things up a bit—she goes all flinty-faced. Shift to sweet, she goes sour. I mean, people can't have their own minds about anything!!! Talk about a free country!!! And the stuff we have to read! Can't believe how stupid and *boring* Jack London is! I mean, really. *The Call of the Wild*. Talk about dogs! Ma says she had to read it when *she* was in school. There has to be better stuff to read for ninth grade somewhere. I thought high school was going to be different.

Have to figure a way to run past Narwin.

10:45 P.M.

From a Letter Written by Margaret Narwin to Her Sister, Anita Wigham

---

Yes, Anita, I suppose that after doing *anything* for twenty-one years a body does get a little tired. And I *have* been teaching English at Harrison High for just that long. All the same, I remain steadfast in my belief that my life was meant to be *the bringing of fine literature to young minds*. When the connection is made—and from time to time it *is* made— it's all worth it. Is it wrong to speak of the work as a calling? Well, teaching *is* almost a religion to me. I will complain from time to time, but—it *is* my life. The truth is, I like it.

But the *other* truth, Anita, is that students today are not what they used to be. There is no love of literature. Not the way you and I learned it from Mother. Young people don't read at all today—outside of school requirements. They come to literature reluctantly at best, fighting me every inch of the way. It's not as if they aren't bright. They *are*. And I like them and their capacity for independence. But the other side of that independence is a lack of caring for anything beyond themselves. If they ask me once more "What's this have to do with *us*?" I think I'll scream. Of course, I don't scream. You have to treat them with care *and* fairness. Fairness is *so* important to them.

For example: these days I'm teaching *The Call of the Wild*.

4

A student raised his hand to say he didn't understand "who was calling who." Now if I were to laugh or mock, he would be insulted. And I would lose him.

This boy, Philip Malloy, is new to me. I met his parents at First Night, and they seem like pleasant folks; they come regularly to PTA meetings. They are educated—she is, anyway. I'm not sure what they do.

But this Philip—an only son, by the way, which may be the problem—is only a middling student, and it's a shame. A nice-looking boy. A boy I like. Intelligent. With real potential. Perhaps that's why he irritates me so—for he shows no desire to strive, to make sacrifices for the betterment of self, the way we were taught. And, oh, my, Anita, so restless! Worst of all, like so many of them, he exhibits *no* desire to learn. No ambition at all! But it's not even *that* I mind so much. No, it's a certain something—a resistance—to accepting the idea that literature is important. For him or anyone! But it is. *It is!* If I could only convince students of that. It's that desire that keeps me going.

I can hear you saying, "Come on down to Florida." Anita, I don't know if I am ready for that yet.

Yes, I could take early retirement. Mr. Benison (Science) is doing so. But then, he's older than I. And he has a wife who works. The truth is, Anita, I would be lost without my books, my teaching, my students.

I had a note from Ethel Truebel! Do you remember her? She used to be in the West Fork Church congregation years ago. It seems . . .

Thursday, March 15

8:05 A.M.

Discussion
in Bernard Lunser's Homeroom Class

MR. LUNSER: Let's go! Let's go! *Carpe diem*. Time to grab the moment!

INTERCOM VOICE OF DR. GERTRUDE DOANE, HARRISON HIGH PRINCIPAL: Good morning to all students, faculty, and staff. Today is Thursday, March 15. Today will be a Schedule A day.

MR. LUNSER: Get that, bozos? A day!

DR. DOANE: Today in history: on this day in 44 B.C., Julius Caesar was assassinated.

MR. LUNSER: And right after that they all sat down and ate a Caesar salad.

DR. DOANE: In 1767, Andrew Jackson, our seventh president, was born.

MR. LUNSER: So by the time this here Andy's term was over, he was four years old.

DR. DOANE: It was in 1820 that Maine was admitted to the United States.

MR. LUNSER: And by 1821 they wanted out.

DR. DOANE: Please all rise and stand at respectful, silent attention for the playing of our national anthem.

Oh, say, can you see by the dawn's early light,
What so proudly we hailed at the twilight's last gleaming? . . .

MR. LUNSER: Okay, Philip, is that yesterday's homework or today's you're working on?

6
∎

Whose broad stripes and bright stars, thro' the perilous
fight . . .

PHILIP MALLOY: I'm trying to pass an exam.

MR. LUNSER: Ah, the famous wit and wisdom of Mr. Malloy.
Philip, I'm the only one allowed to make jokes around
here. Put the book away.

O'er the ramparts we watched were so gallantly streaming? . . .

PHILIP MALLOY: Just one last paragraph?

MR. LUNSER: Away, Philip! Or I'll make you sing along solo!

And the rockets' red glare, the bombs bursting in air,
Gave proof thro' the night that our flag was still there.
Oh, say does that star-spangled banner yet wave
O'er the land of the free and the home of the brave?

MR. LUNSER: Okay. Move it out! Move it out! Hey, and be
careful in those hallways.

STUDENT: What about announcements?

MR. LUNSER: Seems there aren't any, for which we can all
be grateful. Anyway, Philip needs the time to study for
his exam!

11:05 P.M.

From the Diary of Philip Malloy

Winter term exams next week. Hate them. Studying is so
boring! I read the biology book for about twenty minutes
tonight. Then I realized I wasn't really *reading*. Must have
been asleep or something.

Three exams scheduled in one day!!! The trick is getting
past the teacher. It's like a race. You have to have a strat-
egy—know when to take it easy, know when to turn on the

juice. Get teachers to *think* you're in control. Have to know when to kick. Like—put in one of *their* ideas. Or when all else fails make them laugh.

The exam I really want to study for is math. I could get a good mark. People think I'm weird, but I like math.

I won't waste time on English. What can you say about a dog? Besides, it's just a matter of opinion, anyway!!! If I could only get Narwin to crack a smile.

Mom and Dad have been arguing a lot lately. Wonder what *that* means? Dad said his business is in a cash flow squeeze. Mom says the phone company wants employees to pay more into the health plan. Says that's not fair. Dad says the point of business is to make the most money.

Been checking Allison out. She looked cool today. Dad says that when you're a sports star girls really go for you. Hey, Allison, remember me? Phil. Phil Malloy. Right! How would you like a box seat at the Olympics?

Mr. Bentcroft—on Washington Street—owes me for three weeks of newspapers. Talk about dogs!!!!

Sunny at first today. Then cloudy. Bit of rain. Then sunny again. Still, I got in a couple of hours of workout. Mostly wind sprints. Then twenty minutes on Dad's rowing machine.

In *Running* magazine, there's this guy, Steve Hallick, who's 17, and he's doing the 55 meters in 6.51 seconds!!!!

Track team practice season starts next week. Can't wait. That's all Dad and I talk about.

Friday, March 16

MEMO

HARRISON SCHOOL DISTRICT

Where Our Children Are Educated, Not Just Taught

Dr. Albert Seymour
Superintendent

Mrs. Gloria Harland
Chairman, School Board

TO: PHILIP MALLOY
FROM: DR. JOSEPH PALLENI,
      ASSISTANT PRINCIPAL,
      HARRISON HIGH SCHOOL
RE: NEW HOMEROOM ASSIGNMENTS FOR
    SPRING TERM

Dear __Philip__,

    As we head into the Spring term, the faculty committee has made some changes in homeroom assignments. This will facilitate the movements of students, as well as allow for a greater degree of freedom in the planning of Spring term extracurricular schedules.

    Your new homeroom teacher is: __Miss Narwin__, in room: __206__, Effective __Wednesday, March 28, 8 A.M.__

    Thank you for your cooperation.

DR. JOSEPH PALLENI
Assistant Principal

Phone Conversation
between Philip Malloy and Allison Doresett

PHILIP MALLOY: Can I speak to Allison, please?

ALLISON DORESETT: This is she.

PHILIP MALLOY: Oh, Allison. . . . Hi. This is Phil.

ALLISON DORESETT: Phil?

PHILIP MALLOY: Philip Malloy.

ALLISON DORESETT: Oh, hi.

PHILIP MALLOY: What's happening?

ALLISON DORESETT: Not much.

PHILIP MALLOY: Must have been something you ate.

ALLISON DORESETT: Disgusting!

PHILIP MALLOY: Hey, I . . . I was wondering . . . the English exam. Next week. You know? . . .

ALLISON DORESETT: Yes?

PHILIP MALLOY: Well, I thought . . . did you read the whole thing yet? *Call of the Wild.*

ALLISON DORESETT: Finished it last night. We're supposed to review it all tomorrow, you know. For that exam.

PHILIP MALLOY: Allison . . .

ALLISON DORESETT: What?

10
PHILIP MALLOY: I lost my copy.

ALLISON DORESETT: You what?

PHILIP MALLOY: Wasn't my fault. See, I had this idea—I thought I'd try reading it to a dog.

ALLISON DORESETT: A dog!

PHILIP MALLOY: Well, it's about dogs, right? So I started to read it to him—this really mean dog—slobbering mouth, running eyes, the whole bit—only, see, he grabs it and starts to run away.

ALLISON DORESETT: This isn't true. . . .

PHILIP MALLOY: No, listen! Don't laugh! I'm serious! And I chased him into—I'm a runner, right?—chased him into a yard and there he was—burying the book in the ground. I couldn't get it back. The point is, *he* hated it too!

ALLISON DORESETT: You're too much.

PHILIP MALLOY: So, I have to tell Narwin I couldn't finish it.

ALLISON DORESETT: Right. Dare you to say that to her.

PHILIP MALLOY: Think I should?

ALLISON DORESETT: You always make remarks.

PHILIP MALLOY: Somebody's got to keep the class awake.

ALLISON DORESETT: Yeah, but, hate to tell you, I liked the book.

PHILIP MALLOY: Whoops! Sorry, wrong number! Good-bye!

4

Monday, March 19

Excerpt
from Margaret Narwin's Winter Term Exam

Question four: What is the significance of Jack London's choice in making Buck, the dog in *The Call of the Wild*, the focus of his novel? Is the dog meant to be symbolic? Explain your answer. Can *people* learn from this portrayal of a dog? Expand on these ideas.

Philip Malloy's Answer
to Exam-Question Four

The significance of Buck in Jack London's novel *The Call of the Wild* is that Buck is symbolic of a cat. You might think that cats have nothing to do with the book, but *that* is the point. Dogs are willing to sit around and have writers write about them, which, in my personal opinion, makes them dumb. I think cats are smart. Cats don't like cold. A book that takes up so much time about a dog is pretty dumb. The book itself is a dog. That is what people can learn from Jack London's novel *The Call of the Wild*.

Comment by Margaret Narwin
on Philip Malloy's Exam Paper

Philip, this is an unacceptable response. *The Call of the Wild* is an acknowledged masterpiece of American literature. You are not required to like it. You—along with your fellow students—*are* required to give it your *respectful*, thoughtful attention. In short, you are being asked to be more than lazy in your thinking.

Though your other answers are only a little better, I know you have the potential for good work. Your Fall term work showed greater promise, though your classroom attitude leaves much to be desired. Now, Philip, if you do not bring your work up, you are in danger of failing this course. When you get your Winter term grade, consider it a warning.

EXAM GRADE: C–

Tuesday, March 20

MEMO

HARRISON SCHOOL DISTRICT

Where Our Children Are Educated, Not Just Taught

Dr. Albert Seymour
Superintendent

Mrs. Gloria Harland
Chairman, School Board

TO: DR. GERTRUDE DOANE,
     PRINCIPAL, HARRISON HIGH SCHOOL
FROM: MARGARET NARWIN
RE: APPLICATION FOR GRANT

Attached please find my application to the State Office for Education for a summer grant-in-aid.

As you can see, I am applying to the State University for a summer program entitled "New Approaches to the Teaching of Literature for Today's Students."

It's an intensive two-week workshop in which university professors and high school "master teachers" will present new ideas, theoretical as well as practical, for the experienced high school English teacher. The application form requires both an approval and a recommendation from my head administrator, which is why I write you.

I have been teaching for a long time. Indeed, you, Dr. Doane, one of my most successful students, will know how long! I feel I am in need of new ideas, strategies, concepts to keep my teaching vital. The truth is—and I believe I can speak honestly to you about this—I feel that sometimes I am a little out of touch with contemporary teaching, and, just as important, the students who come before me these days. My love of literature—which has served me so well all these years—is perhaps not

14
■

enough. I want to find new works and new ways to entice the young people of today.

In any case, you can easily see that the real beneficiaries of the program—if I am able to attend—will be the students of Harrison High.

I know how reduced and restricted district money is these days, but over the years I have not asked for this kind of support before. The State University tuition, two thousand dollars, is quite beyond my personal budget.

May I ask you to give this request your personal and immediate attention.

Sincerely,

Peg

MARGARET NARWIN

Wednesday, March 21

MEMO

HARRISON SCHOOL DISTRICT

Where Our Children Are Educated, Not Just Taught

Dr. Albert Seymour
Superintendent

Mrs. Gloria Harland
Chairman, School Board

TO: ALL ADMINISTRATORS, FACULTY,
AND STAFF
FROM: SCHOOL SUPERINTENDENT SEYMOUR

Dear Colleagues:

As I am sure you are well aware, the April 5 municipal elections will have voters—*for the second time*—casting ballots on the school budget. This time, in addition, a new Board of Education will be chosen.

Since the budget was rejected a month ago, we have worked very hard to cut our request for next year to the bone. But there is still no guarantee that the voters will accept this budget either.

Throughout the U.S. we find that the aging population (living on restricted and/or shrinking incomes in an inflation-prone world), along with reduced government support of education, conflicts with the needs of young people who live in a society that demands educational excellence even while promoting passive acceptance of mass-media culture.

I therefore *urge* all of you to talk to as many voters as possible in an effort to make clear our vision of the educational future here in Harrison. *Let me be blunt*. A failure to win voter approval on this budget can only mean major problems for programs *and* personnel.

In reference to the forthcoming board elections, I

16
■

should like to remind you of this: tempers can flare; hot words are often part of public debate. If, by chance, any controversial issue springs up between now and election day, I would very much appreciate being informed as to the particulars. None of us likes to be taken unawares. If this office can provide information and facts to the electorate, we shall all be better off. An informed voter is a wise voter. Let us inform the voters with the truth.

Sincerely,
DR. ALBERT SEYMOUR, D.Ed.
School Superintendent

Friday, March 23

10:30 P.M.

From the Diary of Philip Malloy

Got my term grades. Math, an A. Awesome wicked. B– in biology. That's OK too. And I got a C in history, which is cool. All of that stuff is dead anyway. A straight B in health. But then I got a D in English!!! Narwin is so dumb she didn't get the joke.

I'll have to try something different with her. Maybe I should tell her how boring she is. Bad combo—boring teaching and stupid books. What she really wants us to do is put down the things *she* thinks. She wrote that on my exam paper too. Wish I hadn't thrown it out. It *was* funny. Bet Allison would have laughed. And now I'm going to get Narwin for a homeroom teacher too. *Not me.*

Worked out with Mike at the track. Short sprints. Starts. Long runs. Calmed me down. Tryouts for the team on Monday. Can't wait. I know I'll make it. Have to ask the folks to spring for those shoes.

Maybe I'll give up the paper route.

There was this neat show on TV. Really scary. About these guys in Vietnam. Or maybe it was South America. Doesn't matter. Anyway, it has all this stuff about drug fighters and Arab spies. And the Mafia.

Sarah Gloss was reading this book *The Outsiders*. Said it was the best book she ever read. Said she'd give it to me when she was done.

Saw Allison today. Did this thing. Swept off the cap. Big bow. She was trying to keep from cracking up. I'm getting to her. It's neat the way I can figure out what people think of me. Gives me a jump-start.

Tonight went out to this restaurant called Treasure Island.

Seafood place. Dad loves seafood. He said I could have anything on the menu but lobster. Had a couple of hamburgers
and fries. He was sore. I wish people would say what they
mean.

Twenty minutes on the rowing machine.

Steve Hallick ran a mile in four seven!!!! I'd give *anything*
if I could be like him.

MEMO

HARRISON SCHOOL DISTRICT

Where Our Children Are Educated, Not Just Taught

Dr. Albert Seymour
Superintendent

Mrs. Gloria Harland
Chairman, School Board

TO: MARGARET NARWIN
FROM: DR. GERTRUDE DOANE,
      PRINCIPAL, HARRISON HIGH SCHOOL
RE: APPLICATION FOR GRANT

Dear Peg,

As much as I would like to be supportive, and while I can wholeheartedly approve of your desire to take the workshop "New Approaches to the Teaching of Literature for Today's Students," I am afraid I cannot give it formal approval.

The problem, as you may have foreseen, is severely limited district money.

Such funds as are available for teacher support of this nature have already been allocated. In fact, the last of them just went to Kimberly Howard, the music teacher, who will be taking a summer course in Marching Band Techniques, something that will give pleasure to so many people, and, it is hoped, encourage greater attendance at athletic events. School Superintendent Seymour is very high on sports as a community bond. Need I say more?

Finally, with a budget crisis at hand—the budget vote looms large—it's hard to plan anything at this time.

I do want to say, on a personal level, how much I admire your willingness to expand your intellectual and

20
■

teaching horizons. You have always been one of our best teachers, and I know you will continue to be so. If there is any way I can facilitate your taking this course—other than with district funds—please let me know. You can always count on me.

Sincerely,

Gert

DR. GERTRUDE DOANE

11:20 A.M.

Discussion
between Coach Earl Jamison and
Philip Malloy

PHILIP MALLOY: Coach Jamison?

COACH JAMISON: Oh, Phil. Come on in, boy. Nice to see you. Sit down. Make yourself at home.

PHILIP MALLOY: I got your note. You wanted to see me.

COACH JAMISON: Been reading about the Philadelphia Classic Track Meet.

PHILIP MALLOY: Got a great runner from this school in Pittsburgh.

COACH JAMISON: Steve Hallick?

PHILIP MALLOY: Really great. Fast. And strong.

COACH JAMISON: Sure looks it.

PHILIP MALLOY: Coach Jamison . . .

COACH JAMISON: What's that?

PHILIP MALLOY: I've been practicing every day. Working hard. I really have.

COACH JAMISON: Have you? That's great. I heard you were a hard worker. That's the way to do it. Your dad was a runner, wasn't he?

PHILIP MALLOY: Yeah. He was good. Had to quit.

COACH JAMISON: What happened?

PHILIP MALLOY: Family stuff. His father got sick or something. Couldn't stay in college.

COACH JAMISON: Yeah. It's never easy.

PHILIP MALLOY: I'm really up for the tryouts. I got some class shoes. Worked them in. I think we're going to be county champs.

COACH JAMISON: Hope so. Look, Phil, that's what I wanted to talk to you about. I've got a copy of your winter term grades here.

PHILIP MALLOY: You do?

COACH JAMISON: Well, I have to check these things. Saves problems later on. You know, there's a school rule— actually, a district rule—that you can't be on a team unless you've got a passing grade in every subject. A passing grade.

PHILIP MALLOY: A passing grade?

COACH JAMISON: Yeah. In high school. A passing grade.

PHILIP MALLOY: I didn't know.

COACH JAMISON: Well, high school . . . The point is, Phil, see, here—look—it looks like you don't have—see—all passing grades. Look here, now. There's a D here.

PHILIP MALLOY: I never heard that rule.

COACH JAMISON: In your student handbook. Read it?

PHILIP MALLOY: I don't think anyone does.

COACH JAMISON: *This* grade isn't too bad. And this grade. Fine. These. The one that really hurts is here. English. Now, if you could have gotten that up a notch. Just a bit. Even a C minus. But a D isn't—by the rules—passing. So I guess we've got a problem.

PHILIP MALLOY: We do?

COACH JAMISON: Afraid so. Look—

PHILIP MALLOY: It's Miss Narwin. I keep trying to get her to like me. She won't. She's so old-fashioned. Boring.

COACH JAMISON: Now, Phil. I know she's tough. Is there any point in your talking to her?

PHILIP MALLOY: Me?

COACH JAMISON: Sure.

PHILIP MALLOY: Could you?

COACH JAMISON: What about your doing extra work? I mean, it's no good this way.

PHILIP MALLOY: What do you mean?

COACH JAMISON: The rule . . . As it stands now, Phil—it's not me saying this, but this rule—you're not even allowed to try out. And I'm not going to kid you. This does mess with the team.

PHILIP MALLOY: Honest. I didn't know about that rule.

COACH JAMISON: Exactly. You need passing grades. See, rule's been around for a long time.

PHILIP MALLOY: No one ever told me. And I'm practicing every day.

COACH JAMISON: Sure—

PHILIP MALLOY: It's so unfair.

COACH JAMISON: Well, in high school—

PHILIP MALLOY: I mean, you can't kid around with her or anything.

23
■

COACH JAMISON: Phil, if there is one thing sports teaches—and I'm always saying this—all the guys will tell you—sometimes you have to go along to get along. That's the whole thing about sports. Go with the flow.

PHILIP MALLOY: I think it's a personal thing with her. It really is. She has it in for me. I mean, I shouldn't be in her class. Could you get me switched?

COACH JAMISON: Maybe if you talked to her. Do some catch-up work. How about it? Promise to hit the books. Extra stuff. Bet you could. Look, everything I've heard suggests you are fast. Real potential. This is a big disappointment.

PHILIP MALLOY: I mean, if I knew it was a rule—

COACH JAMISON: Yeah. One thing sports teaches. A rule is a rule. It isn't always easy.

PHILIP MALLOY: I didn't know.

COACH JAMISON: Well, thing is, now you do.

1:30 P.M.

Discussion in
Margaret Narwin's English Class

MISS NARWIN: Now, class, during the first few weeks of this new term we'll be reading William Shakespeare's *Julius Caesar*. How many of you have ever read a play by Shakespeare before? Well, then, you're in for a treat. You are not an educated person unless you have read Shakespeare. Philip?

PHILIP MALLOY: What?

MISS NARWIN: I'd rather you look up at me, not out the window.

PHILIP MALLOY: I was listening.

MISS NARWIN: Can you repeat what I said?

PHILIP MALLOY: We're reading something.

MISS NARWIN: William Shakespeare.

PHILIP MALLOY: Whatever you say.

MISS NARWIN: Philip, I think I've suggested before that your comments can be tiresome. Now, please, try to stay with me.

PHILIP MALLOY: Yeah.

9

Tuesday, March 27

Discussion
between Philip Malloy's Parents

MRS. MALLOY: Honey, did you have a chance to look at Phil's grades?

MR. MALLOY: What?

MRS. MALLOY: Did you look at Phil's grades. I left them on the bureau.

MR. MALLOY: Uh, yes. Where is he?

MRS. MALLOY: In the basement. On your rowing machine.

MR. MALLOY: Should use that thing more myself. Putting on weight.

MRS. MALLOY: You certainly are. Did you?

MR. MALLOY: I'm looking at them now.

MRS. MALLOY: What do you think?

MR. MALLOY: Not too bad. Except for English. What's the problem there?

MRS. MALLOY: He says it's the teacher.

MR. MALLOY: I've seen him read.

MRS. MALLOY: He's reading some paperback. *Insiders. Outsiders.* I don't know. Some girl gave it to him. That doesn't seem to be the problem.

MR. MALLOY: I never was one for reading much. I mean, other than sports. Course now, papers. Too much of that.

MRS. MALLOY: Ben, he could flunk that course.

26
■

MR. MALLOY: Won't be the end of the world. What would he have to do, go to summer school? Maybe that's the lesson he needs. Kids only do what they want to do.

MRS. MALLOY: The last couple of days he's been very moody.

MR. MALLOY: Come on. He's fourteen.

MRS. MALLOY: He doesn't want to talk. To me, anyway. Maybe you should be spending more time with him.

MR. MALLOY: I know. All tied up in this—

MRS. MALLOY: I understand. But work's better, isn't it?

MR. MALLOY: Some. Did he make the track team?

MRS. MALLOY: You know, I completely forgot to ask him. Maybe that's the problem.

MR. MALLOY: I'll talk to him.

MRS. MALLOY: Do you know—about a week ago, he asked me if we—you and I—were getting a divorce?

MR. MALLOY: *What?*

MRS. MALLOY: Really.

MR. MALLOY: How'd he come up with that?

MRS. MALLOY: I'm not sure. Maybe he overheard. . . . I told him bickering happens in a marriage. It's perfectly normal. Life isn't a sitcom.

MR. MALLOY: Right. The real world doesn't have a laugh track.

Discussion
between Philip Malloy and His Father

MR. MALLOY: Can I talk to you?

PHILIP MALLOY: Sure.

MR. MALLOY: How much time you spending on this?

PHILIP MALLOY: Few times a day. Short sprints.

MR. MALLOY: Like I'm always telling you, just make sure you warm up each time. But it's good for the back. Helps with starts.

PHILIP MALLOY: I know.

MR. MALLOY: Uh, Phil . . . School stuff. Straight up. What's the story in English?

PHILIP MALLOY: What do you mean?

MR. MALLOY: I saw your grades. Most of them are decent. What's with English?

PHILIP MALLOY: I can speak it.

MR. MALLOY: Seriously. . . .

PHILIP MALLOY: You want the truth?

MR. MALLOY: Sure. Well?

PHILIP MALLOY: It's the teacher, Narwin.

MR. MALLOY: What do you mean?

PHILIP MALLOY: She has it in for me.

MR. MALLOY: How come?

PHILIP MALLOY: I don't know. Nobody likes her. People don't do well in her classes. Except her favorites.

MR. MALLOY: Want me or your ma to go in and talk to her?

28

PHILIP MALLOY: I can handle her.

MR. MALLOY: What are you reading in school?

PHILIP MALLOY: *Julius Caesar.* Shakespeare.

MR. MALLOY: Uh-oh.

PHILIP MALLOY: *So* bad. This Narwin has us reading these
tiny bits every night, but *no one* understands it. I mean
it, *no one*!!! She says it's English, but it must have been
English before the English got there. At least it's not any
English I've ever heard.

MR. MALLOY: Well, reading is important.

PHILIP MALLOY: I read. Ever hear of *The Outsiders*? It's
about these guys—they live alone— without parents.

MR. MALLOY: Think I saw it on cable. How you getting on
with the track team? Phil?

PHILIP MALLOY: I, ah . . . was thinking I wouldn't try out.

MR. MALLOY: Come again?

PHILIP MALLOY: Thinking of not trying out.

MR. MALLOY: You kidding?

PHILIP MALLOY: No.

MR. MALLOY: But high school track is . . . Why?

PHILIP MALLOY: Lot of reasons.

MR. MALLOY: Like what?

PHILIP MALLOY: Dad . . .

MR. MALLOY: I want to know.

PHILIP MALLOY: Just because you did it doesn't mean I
have to.

MR. MALLOY: Now, wait a minute. You're really into it. We
just got you new shoes. And you're good. Better than I
ever was. You *are.* I love watching you run. You shouldn't
give it up. And here you are working out. I don't get it.
What's going on?

PHILIP MALLOY: Nothing.

MR. MALLOY: Didn't you tell me the coach *asked* you to be on the team?

PHILIP MALLOY: Doesn't mean—

MR. MALLOY: Phil, I don't get it.

PHILIP MALLOY: It's my choice.

MR. MALLOY: Phil, let me tell you something. If God gives you a ticket, you better use it.

PHILIP MALLOY: Ticket to what?

MR. MALLOY: Running.

PHILIP MALLOY: I'll think about it.

MR. MALLOY: Those shoes weren't cheap either. Real first-class stuff. I mean, I don't understand. I thought you were ready for it.

PHILIP MALLOY: Come on, Dad. I'm not you.

9:24 P.M.

From a Letter Written by Margaret Narwin to Her Sister, Anita Wigham

---

. . . Anita, the truth is I'm hurt. *Never* in all the years I've been at Harrison have I asked for *anything* in the way of extra funds. If it were a case of *no* money available for *anyone*, why, I could accept that. But, no, a certain Kimberly Howard, who has been here for only *two* years, and who has a husband who works for some large corporation, *she* received money! And for some idiotic course in marching-band music! It makes me *outraged* to think about it.

What has happened to our society? Where are its values? I suppose marching bands make a big show. Bread and circuses, Anita. Bread and circuses. That's all it is. I don't think I've ever been so angry!

I think there's a question of fairness here. That old-fashioned word *respect*—how often Mother used it!—occurs to me often these days. Call it pride, call it vanity, but I would like some respect for all I have done here. From the community. From the administration. Yes, from the *students*. I work hard for them!

The truth is it's our superintendent's doing. There is a second budget vote coming up. I told you the first one failed. He sent out a memo to everybody warning us that it might fail again. Almost a threat. He is a *very* political person. But then, all he wants is to keep *his* job.

Oh, I am so angry. . . .

10:40 P.M.

From the Diary of Philip Malloy

Folks got my grades. Ma asked me a few things about them before supper. I didn't say much. Then, afterward, Dad talked to me. About the grades. Wasn't that he blew his stack or anything. I told him the truth. He seemed to understand. But then he asked me about my being on the track team. Didn't know what to say. If I told him what happened he would have been really mad. So I just said I decided I wouldn't go for the tryouts.

That got him upset.

I just realized two things that make me want to puke. Track practice starts tomorrow and I'm *not* on the team. Also, I start homeroom with *Narwin*!!!!! Can't stand even looking at her. I have to find a way to get transferred out.

31
∎

Discussion
between Philip Malloy's Parents

MRS. MALLOY: Did you talk to Philip? About that grade?

MR. MALLOY: Sure.

MRS. MALLOY: What's going on?

MR. MALLOY: I'm not sure. Fussing with the English teacher.

MRS. MALLOY: What do you mean?

MR. MALLOY: Like he told you. He doesn't like her. I told him he didn't have much choice. Take the bad with the good. Then he said he wasn't going to try out for track.

MRS. MALLOY: That he was *not*?

MR. MALLOY: That's what he told me.

MRS. MALLOY: But that's all he thinks about.

MR. MALLOY: I know. He doesn't know how good he is. I reminded him.

MRS. MALLOY: Did he give a reason?

MR. MALLOY: Not really. Something about not having to do what I did.

MRS. MALLOY: Oh, he'll change his mind. Kids are so moody.

MR. MALLOY: Hope so.

MRS. MALLOY: Maybe just don't mention it.

MR. MALLOY: Maybe.

MRS. MALLOY: I'm glad you spoke to him. Not every father would.

MR. MALLOY: He doesn't make it easy.

32
∎

10

Wednesday, March 28

7:30 A.M.

Conversation
between Philip Malloy and Ken Barchet
on the Way to the School Bus

PHILIP MALLOY: What's happening, man?

KEN BARCHET: Nothing. Got room changes. Who'd you get?

PHILIP MALLOY: Narwin.

KEN BARCHET: So do I. She's okay.

PHILIP MALLOY: Can't stand her.

KEN BARCHET: Doesn't matter. It's just homeroom.

PHILIP MALLOY.   No way. I've got her for English too. I'm going to get transferred out of both.

KEN BARCHET: Why?

PHILIP MALLOY: Told you. Can't stand her.

KEN BARCHET: How you going to do that?

PHILIP MALLOY: I'm working on it.

KEN BARCHET: Sure . . . Malloy Magic, right?

PHILIP MALLOY: You'll see.

Discussion
in Margaret Narwin's Homeroom Class

MISS NARWIN: Ladies and gentlemen, please settle down. All right. Settle down. For the moment just take any seat you wish. We'll work out particular problems a bit later on. Yes?

STUDENT: Am I supposed to be in this room?

MISS NARWIN: What's your name?

STUDENT: Lisa Gibbons.

MISS NARWIN: Lisa? Yes, you're on my list. Just take any seat for the moment.

STUDENT: Miss Narwin, what about me?

MISS NARWIN: Is that you, Gloria? No, you're not here. Did you get a notice?

GLORIA: No.

MISS NARWIN: Oh, dear. Best check in the main office.

ALLISON DORESETT: What about me?

MISS NARWIN: You'll all have to lower your voices if I'm going to sort things out. Yes, Allison, you are here. Yes?

STUDENT: Joseph R. Rippens.

MISS NARWIN: I think that—

INTERCOM VOICE OF DR. GERTRUDE DOANE, HARRISON HIGH PRINCIPAL: Good morning to all students, faculty, and staff.

STUDENT: Am I?

MISS NARWIN: Please, let's just get done with the morning business.

34
■

DR. DOANE: Today is Wednesday, March 28. Today will be a Schedule B day.

Today in history: in the year A.D. 193 the Roman Emperor Pertinax was assassinated. On this day in 1862 the Civil War battle of Glorieta, New Mexico, was fought. Today in Czechoslovakia it is Teachers' Day.

Please all rise and stand at respectful, silent attention for the playing of our national anthem.

Oh, say, can you see by the dawn's early light . . .

MISS NARWIN: Is that someone humming?

What so proudly we hailed at the twilight's last gleaming?
Whose broad stripes and bright stars . . .

MISS NARWIN: I don't know who that is, but you heard Dr. Doane request silence.

. . . thro' the perilous fight,
O'er the ramparts we watched were so gallantly streaming? . . .

MISS NARWIN: Is that you, Philip?

And the rockets' red glare, the bombs bursting in air . . .

PHILIP MALLOY: Just humming.

MISS NARWIN: Please stop it.

Gave proof thro' the night that our flag was still there. . . .

PHILIP MALLOY: Mr. Lunser doesn't mind. I just—

MISS NARWIN: Stop it now.

PHILIP MALLOY: But—

Oh, say does that star-spangled banner yet wave . . .

MISS NARWIN: Now! Thank you.

O'er the land of the free and the home of the brave?   35
∎

Discussion between Margaret Narwin and
Jacob Benison, Science Teacher,
in the Faculty Room

MR. BENISON: Morning, Peg. How's it going? Lots of confusion with the new homerooms?

MISS NARWIN: I'll get through it.

MR. BENISON: Awful lot of mix-ups. Kids going every which way. As if they weren't informed. Happens this way every year. Sometimes I think it's not worth the trouble.

MISS NARWIN: I agree.

MR. BENISON: I'll be glad to get out of it. Forty-four more days!

MISS NARWIN: Sometimes I think I should join you.

MR. BENISON: Can't wait. Get you some coffee? Kim brought in muffins.

MISS NARWIN: Kim?

MR. BENISON: Kimberly Howard. Music.

MISS NARWIN: I'll just sit here.

MR. BENISON: Something the matter, Peg?

MISS NARWIN: Oh, stupid business. I suppose it's this changing homeroom classes. The announcements, and so on. And when the national anthem comes on, the students *are* supposed to stand in silence.

36
■

MR. BENISON: Right. "Respect, silence, and attention," I think the rule reads.

MISS NARWIN: Exactly. I had a student who started to hum loudly. Very loudly.

MR. BENISON: Uh-oh. Who was that?

MISS NARWIN: Philip Malloy.

MR. BENISON: Oh, sure, Phil. Nice kid. Bright—when he gets around to doing some work. Which isn't exactly every day. He's got being fast on his brain. Humming loudly? What was he doing that for?

MISS NARWIN: I don't know. I had to ask him to stop.

MR. BENISON: Did he?

MISS NARWIN: Not at first. I spoke to him twice. He claimed he always did it before.

MR. BENISON: That right?

MISS NARWIN: Bernie Lunser's class.

MR. BENISON: Oh? Well, the term won't last forever.

MISS NARWIN: Sometimes I wonder. Maybe I will get some coffee.

MR. BENISON: Hey, the meaning of life!

12:15 P.M.

Discussion
between Philip Malloy and Todd Becker
in the School Lunchroom

TODD BECKER: Hey, man, how come you aren't going out for track?

PHILIP MALLOY: Got too much to do.

TODD BECKER: We could use you, man. Need some power. We really could.

PHILIP MALLOY: I'll think about it.

TODD BECKER: You should.

PHILIP MALLOY: Just don't bug me.

TODD BECKER: Sure. Sure. I'm just asking. Who'd you get for homeroom?

PHILIP MALLOY: What?

TODD BECKER: Who's your new homeroom teacher?

PHILIP MALLOY: Narwin.

TODD BECKER: I like her.

PHILIP MALLOY: I hate her.

TODD BECKER: Yeah? How come?

PHILIP MALLOY: She is the stupidest teacher. . . . You know how they play "The Star-Spangled Banner" in the morning . . . ?

TODD BECKER: Yeah. . . .

PHILIP MALLOY: Well, I started to sing it. . . .

TODD BECKER: Why?

PHILIP MALLOY: Felt like it.

TODD BECKER: So?

PHILIP MALLOY: She told me to stop.

TODD BECKER: Stop what?

PHILIP MALLOY: Humming.

TODD BECKER: Thought you said singing.

PHILIP MALLOY: Whatever.

TODD BECKER: How come she made you stop?

PHILIP MALLOY: I don't know. She's got something against me. I don't know what it is. She really has it in for me. Something. I mean, she's always onto me about something. Really. I wish I knew.

TODD BECKER: What did you do?

PHILIP MALLOY: I told you. Nothing.

TODD BECKER: No. I mean when she told you to stop humming.

PHILIP MALLOY: I stopped.

TODD BECKER: Man, those are the biggest cookies I ever saw. Like pizzas.

PHILIP MALLOY: My mother makes them.

TODD BECKER: Amazing.

PHILIP MALLOY: Here. Take a piece. Humming, would you believe it? No way I'm staying in her classes.

1:40 P.M.

Discussion
in Margaret Narwin's English Class

MISS NARWIN: Now, scene two, line fifty-two. Brutus says, "No, Cassius; for the eye sees not itself / But by reflection, by some other things." What does he mean by that? Anyone? Someone want to take a chance? Roger?

ROGER SANCHEZ: That he can't see himself.

MISS NARWIN: Close. Yes, Philip?

PHILIP MALLOY: Yeah, but what if he's cross-eyed? He'd see himself then, wouldn't he?

MISS NARWIN: Philip, I'm not even going to respond to that! Terri?

Discussion
between Philip Malloy and Allison Doresett
on the School Bus

ALLISON DORESETT: Can I sit next to you?

PHILIP MALLOY: Oh, sure. Sure.

ALLISON DORESETT: What's the matter? You look like death warmed over.

PHILIP MALLOY: I'm okay.

ALLISON DORESETT: You got Miss Narwin mad with that joke in English.

PHILIP MALLOY: She's always mad at me.

ALLISON DORESETT: Is something the matter?

PHILIP MALLOY: Nothing.

ALLISON DORESETT: School was so frantic today.

PHILIP MALLOY: Yeah.

ALLISON DORESETT: All the sports and stuff. Hey, how come you didn't go to track tryouts?

PHILIP MALLOY: Had to do something.

ALLISON DORESETT: Todd said you were really great. That with you on the team we were going to be county champs.

PHILIP MALLOY: Yeah.

ALLISON DORESETT: Boy, you're in a mood!

PHILIP MALLOY: Just don't feel like talking.

ALLISON DORESETT: Well *excuse* me!

PHILIP MALLOY: Hey, Allison, wait . . . Damn!

40

Discussion between
Margaret Narwin and Bernard Lunser
Outside the School's Main Office

MISS NARWIN: Bernie!

MR. LUNSER: Oh, hi, Peg. How you doing?

MISS NARWIN: Fine. I need to ask you something.

MR. LUNSER: What's that?

MISS NARWIN: In your morning homeroom . . .

MR. LUNSER: Yeah?

MISS NARWIN: When the national anthem is played . . .

MR. LUNSER: Right . . .

MISS NARWIN: Do you allow your students to sing along?

MR. LUNSER: Sing?

MISS NARWIN: During the national anthem.

MR. LUNSER: Ummmmmm . . . I thought the kids are supposed to be quiet.

MISS NARWIN: One of my new homeroom students, Philip
Malloy, informed me that you always allowed singing.

MR. LUNSER: Oh, Philip . . . Right. He was in my homeroom. He'd do better if he thought himself a little less
clever and got his brain into something besides running.
But I like him. A decent kid. You get him?

MISS NARWIN: Do you allow singing?

MR. LUNSER: Singing?

MISS NARWIN: Yes.

MR. LUNSER: The rule says keep quiet. . . .

MISS NARWIN: But do you allow singing?

MR. LUNSER: Hey, Peg, do I look like a guy who goes around breaking important rules?

MISS NARWIN: Thanks.

7:15 P.M.

Discussion
between Philip Malloy and His Parents
During Dinner

MRS. MALLOY: You seem very quiet tonight, Philip. Want some more gravy?

PHILIP MALLOY: I've got enough.

MR. MALLOY: I'll have some. What did you decide to do about the track team?

MRS. MALLOY: Philip, your father asked you something.

PHILIP MALLOY: What?

MR. MALLOY: I asked you a question. You still not going out for track?

MRS. MALLOY: Philip, is something the matter?

PHILIP MALLOY: I'm not on the team.

MR. MALLOY: I know that's what you said. But I'd like to know why. Something must be the matter.

PHILIP MALLOY: What would you say . . .

MRS. MALLOY: Phil, don't talk with your mouth full.

MR. MALLOY: Have I *ever* missed one of your meets? Ever? This boy is the best runner in town. Makes me feel proud.

42
■

MRS. MALLOY: Ben, we know that. What were you saying, Phil?

PHILIP MALLOY: What would you say if a teacher said I wasn't allowed to sing "The Star-Spangled Banner"?

MR. MALLOY: What?

PHILIP MALLOY: Singing "The Star-Spangled Banner."

MR. MALLOY: Anywhere?

PHILIP MALLOY: In class.

MRS. MALLOY: I don't understand. What's this have to do with what your father asked—your running? Singing in the middle of class?

PHILIP MALLOY: Ma, listen! I'm trying to tell you. I mean . . . you know, when school starts, first period, home-room, when they play, you know, the . . . song over the speaker system. It's a tape.

MR. MALLOY: Come again.

PHILIP MALLOY: I'm trying to explain!

MR. MALLOY: No need to raise your voice!

MRS. MALLOY: The both of you . . .

MR. MALLOY: Now, Philip, just tell us what—obviously, something has happened. Calmly and factually, tell us what happened. Why you are so upset?

PHILIP MALLOY: I told you. . . . In school today . . .

MR. MALLOY: Okay. In school today. But what?

PHILIP MALLOY: We got new homeroom teachers.

MRS. MALLOY: Just you?

PHILIP MALLOY: No. I never said that. Everybody. The whole school.

MRS. MALLOY: I don't understand.

MR. MALLOY: Susan, just let Phil tell his story without in-terruptions.

MRS. MALLOY: I'm just trying to understand.

PHILIP MALLOY: Anyway, I got this Miss Narwin. She's a real bitch. . . .

MR. MALLOY: Phil!

PHILIP MALLOY: Do you want to know what happened or not!

MRS. MALLOY: Honey, let the boy tell it his way.

PHILIP MALLOY: Anyway, they always start off the day, you know, with playing "The Star-Spangled Banner." Okay. It's stupid, but, well, sometimes I sort of sing along. . . .

MRS. MALLOY: You have a very sweet voice.

PHILIP MALLOY: Or hum. . . .

MR. MALLOY: Hum?

PHILIP MALLOY: Yeah. Right. Hum. No big deal. But this teacher, she got real mad and started to yell at me to stop.

MRS. MALLOY: She yelled?

PHILIP MALLOY: Yeah.

MR. MALLOY: Let me understand this. Just—out of the blue—she yelled at you because you were—?

PHILIP MALLOY: Right. Humming. That's all I was doing, I mean, not loud. Soft.

MR. MALLOY: And she yelled at you?

PHILIP MALLOY: That's what I'm trying to say.

MRS. MALLOY: That's not what I'd call fair.

44
■

MR. MALLOY: The national anthem—"Oh, say, can you see"—is that what you're talking about?

PHILIP MALLOY: Yeah.

MR. MALLOY: You have some more of that . . . ?

MRS. MALLOY: Yams. Sweet yams.

MR. MALLOY: Thanks. They're delicious. Now where is he going?

MRS. MALLOY: He was trying to talk, and you weren't listening to him. Ben, you have to be more supportive!

MR. MALLOY: What do you mean?

MRS. MALLOY: Maybe that's why he isn't running. Maybe he's sending a message.

MR. MALLOY: Like what?

MRS. MALLOY: That he needs your support on something that isn't track. That's him.

MR. MALLOY: Think so?

MRS. MALLOY: I don't know. Just trying to understand.

MR. MALLOY: My day wasn't so great either.

MRS. MALLOY: Oh?

MR. MALLOY: Remember that bid we put in on that Colfax job? . . .

8:32 P.M.

From a Letter Written by Margaret Narwin to Her Sister, Anita Wigham

---

. . . I do think it's quite the best thing Barbara Pym ever wrote. It's one of those books about which—even as I neared the end—I said to myself, "I can't wait to read this again."

In any case, it was so soothing to come home to that quiet, thoughtful, civilized British world. Oh, Anita, I *long* to return to England someday, and those wonderful, leisurely late-afternoon cream teas. . . .

The truth is, I needed a soothing. Today was "Spring Changeover Day," when our students, after six months of struggling to learn exactly where to go, are suddenly tossed pell-mell here, there, anywhere, as their schedules and home-room assignments shift because of spring recreational schedules. Of course, bedlam is *always* the result, with attendant bad feeling. It's just at those moments that students rear up and challenge your authority. One has to be vigilant and *firm*. As well as consistent and fair. That's the key with students these days. And sometimes I haven't the stamina for it. Ah, well . . .

Thank you for passing on the kind words of Mr. Chevers. Of course I remember him. . . .

9:05 P.M.

From the Diary of Philip Malloy

Today was rotten. Nothing was right. I felt like punching Narwin in the face. It all just stinks.

9:20 P.M.

Phone Conversation
between Allison Doresett and Janet Barsky

ALLISON DORESETT: Oh, on the bus coming home, you know, I was going to sit with Phil Malloy.

JANET BARSKY: You like him, don't you?

ALLISON DORESETT: He's kind of cute. And usually really funny. But he looked upset today. Angry.

JANET BARSKY: How come?

ALLISON DORESETT: I don't know. He was that way in class too. I tried to talk to him, but he wouldn't. Anyway, I didn't sit with him.

JANET BARSKY: Who'd you sit with?

ALLISON DORESETT: Todd Becker.

JANET BARSKY: Todd! Too cool! He's the cutest guy!

ALLISON DORESETT: I know. . . . And he *always* makes me laugh.

10:45 P.M.

Conversation
between Philip Malloy and His Father

MR. MALLOY: Phil? You up? Can I speak to you?

PHILIP MALLOY: Oh, sure. Just reading.

MR. MALLOY: What're you reading?

PHILIP MALLOY: *The Outsiders.*

MR. MALLOY: Still?

PHILIP MALLOY: It's pretty long.

MR. MALLOY: Can I sit down?

PHILIP MALLOY: Sure.

MR. MALLOY: Now, look, this business about, you know, what you were saying at dinner, not being allowed to sing the national anthem . . .

PHILIP MALLOY: I was humming.

MR. MALLOY: Whatever. Now, your mother and I talked about this. I mean, I want you to understand—whatever it is—we're on your side.

PHILIP MALLOY: I didn't think you were interested.

MR. MALLOY: Of course I'm interested. I'm always cheering on your side.

PHILIP MALLOY: It's just that the teacher—

47

MR. MALLOY: No, wait. Straight up. I think she's wrong. No two ways about it. You're right to be bugged. She shouldn't put you down like that. You know, I'm—your mother and I—we're no great, well, you know, no big patriots. I don't think we even own a flag. But that doesn't mean we don't love our country. Believe me. We just don't make a big thing about it. It's not that kind of showy thing with us. But not being allowed to sing "The Star-Spangled Banner" . . . Well, that's like, sort of, not being allowed to, you know, pray. A personal thing. And the personal thing, in America . . . the point is, it doesn't seem right. And we just want you to know we're with you. It's important to us that you know that.

PHILIP MALLOY: Thanks.

MR. MALLOY: Your mother says to be more supportive. Well, sure. I mean, I'll stand with you. You never have to worry about that.

PHILIP MALLOY: You're not mad?

MR. MALLOY: Of course not. I have half a mind to talk to Ted.

PHILIP MALLOY: Why?

MR. MALLOY: He's running for school board. Election soon. I mean, Ted Griffen *is* our neighbor. That can mean something.

PHILIP MALLOY: He was always chasing me off his lawn.

MR. MALLOY: Yeah. But you were a kid then. Phil, let me tell you something. One thing I've learned is this: you really have to stick up for your rights. We'll stand with you. Don't worry. See you at breakfast.

48
.

PHILIP MALLOY: Right.

MR. MALLOY: Night, kid.

PHILIP MALLOY: Night.

MR. MALLOY: Remember. You stick up for your rights. I'll be there.

11

Thursday, March 29

8:02 A.M.

Discussion
in Margaret Narwin's Homeroom Class

MISS NARWIN: Ladies and gentlemen, please take your seats. Your assigned seats. I need to take attendance.

STUDENT: Miss Narwin.

MISS NARWIN: Yes?

STUDENT: Peggy Lord is sick.

MISS NARWIN: Thank you.

INTERCOM VOICE OF DR. GERTRUDE DOANE, HARRISON HIGH PRINCIPAL: Good morning to all students, faculty, and staff. Today is Thursday, March 29. Today will be a Schedule A day.

Today in history: in the year 1790 our tenth president, John Tyler, was born. In 1918 singer Pearl Bailey was born. And today in 1954 Karen Ann Quinlan was born.

Please all rise and stand at respectful, silent attention for the playing of our national anthem.

Oh, say, can you see by the dawn's early light . . .

MISS NARWIN: Is that someone humming?

What so proudly we hailed at the twilight's last gleaming?
Whose broad stripes and bright stars . . .

MISS NARWIN: Philip, is that you again?

. . . thro' the perilous fight,
O'er the ramparts we watched were so gallantly streaming? . . .

MISS NARWIN: Philip, I spoke to you yesterday about this.

49
■

And the rockets' red glare, the bombs bursting in air . . .

MISS NARWIN: This is a time for listening. Now, please, *stop* singing.

Gave proof thro' the night that our flag was still there. . . .

MISS NARWIN: Philip, stop this insolence!

Oh, say does that star-spangled banner yet wave
O'er the land of the free and the home of the brave?

MISS NARWIN: Philip, leave this room instantly. Report to Dr. Palleni's office. Now!

8:35 A.M.

Conversation between
Philip Malloy and Dr. Joseph Palleni,
Assistant Principal, Harrison High

DR. PALLENI: Okay, Philip, come on in. Sit yourself down. Who's your homeroom teacher?

PHILIP MALLOY: Miss Narwin.

DR. PALLENI: Okay. Now, what seems to be the problem?

PHILIP MALLOY: I don't know.

DR. PALLENI: Come on, Phil. Sit up straight. We don't whip people here. Now, you must have some idea. She asked you to leave the class. What happened?

PHILIP MALLOY: She doesn't like me.

50   DR. PALLENI: Let's try to be more specific, Philip. I want to hear your side of the problem. I'll check with her. Then, let's see if we can work something out. We're into solving problems, not making them. Okay. Now, what happened?

PHILIP MALLOY: She wouldn't let me sing "The Star-Spangled Banner."

DR. PALLENI: What?

PHILIP MALLOY: She won't let me sing "The Star-Spangled Banner."

DR. PALLENI: I don't understand.

PHILIP MALLOY: It's just a thing I like to do. Sing along when the song is played.

DR. PALLENI: "The Star-Spangled Banner"?

PHILIP MALLOY: Yeah. I just like to do it. In Mr. Lunser's—

DR. PALLENI: You mean—when the morning tape plays . . . ?

PHILIP MALLOY: Yeah.

DR. PALLENI: And you were singing?

PHILIP MALLOY: Uh-huh.

DR. PALLENI: What, loudly? Disrespectfully? Were you making fun?

PHILIP MALLOY: No. Not at all. Just, you know, sort of to myself. Almost humming. Really. I always do.

DR. PALLENI: There's a rule about being quiet at that time.

PHILIP MALLOY: Yeah, well, it's sort of a . . . patriotic thing with me. But the whole thing is, she always has it in for me.

DR. PALLENI: Who?

PHILIP MALLOY: Narwin. So, she kicked me out.

DR. PALLENI: This singing you were doing . . . singing out loud. Did Miss Narwin ask you to stop?

PHILIP MALLOY: I mean, I wasn't being loud or anything like that.

DR. PALLENI: And did you? Stop, I mean.

PHILIP MALLOY: No, I told you. I was singing.

DR. PALLENI: But, when she—Miss Narwin—asked you, did you stop?

PHILIP MALLOY: It was just to myself. Not loud or anything, and—

DR. PALLENI: Okay, okay, Phil. I think I understand now. No problem. Where is that thing? . . . Here it is. This is a memo from Dr. Doane. Look, see what it says. Go on, read it. What does it say? *Silent.* Okay? You hear it every day. Right? But you were singing. Right? No, let me finish. Miss Narwin asked you to stop. You didn't. You continued to sing. You were disobedient. So she asked you to leave.

PHILIP MALLOY: How can you ask someone not to sing "The Star-Spangled Banner"?

DR. PALLENI: It's the rule.

PHILIP MALLOY: Is a memo a rule?

DR. PALLENI: Philip . . .

PHILIP MALLOY: Yeah, but . . .

DR. PALLENI: Philip, look. I've got more important things to do with my time than argue with you about following simple, basic rules. I've got serious infractions. I've got drugs. I've got—

PHILIP MALLOY: Put me in another homeroom.

DR. PALLENI: What?

PHILIP MALLOY: Put me in another homeroom. And another English class.

DR. PALLENI: What's English have to do with this? Philip, I asked you something.

PHILIP MALLOY: She and I don't get along.

DR. PALLENI: Look, Phil, you are here to get an education. To get along you have to go along. Let's not make a big deal over this, okay, Phil? Now, you've given me your side of the story. I'll check with Miss Narwin, but it seems pretty clear to me. . . . You said yourself, you broke a rule—

PHILIP MALLOY: If you could just change . . .

DR. PALLENI: Here's a note that says I spoke to you. Scoot. Get along with your day. Make it a good one.

PHILIP MALLOY: But . . .

DR. PALLENI: Hey, Phil, be cool. It's a good day. I heard you're a runner. It's a great day for running. Go join the track team. They could use you. Okay? Now, take it easy. See you around. Bye. Have a nice day.

1:35 P.M.

Conversation
between Mr. Malloy and His Boss,
Mr. Dexter

MR. DEXTER: Look, Ben, it was just a botched job, that's all. There are no two ways around it.

MR. MALLOY: Mr. Dexter, what I'm simply trying to explain is that I wasn't given all the information that would allow me—

MR. DEXTER: I don't want to hear excuses, Ben. I want someone around here to accept responsibility. Is that you or not?

MR. MALLOY: Yes, sir.

MR. DEXTER: It goes with your position. Responsibility. Just don't let it happen again. We lost a lot of money on this one. We can't afford it. No one should know that better than you.

MR. MALLOY: Yes, sir.

MR. DEXTER: Okay. That's all that needs to be said. It's done. We'll work around it.

MR. MALLOY: Yes, sir.

MR. DEXTER: Regular sales-reps meeting tomorrow morning. I don't intend to bring this up. But it will be on my mind. We can't afford another screwup.

MR. MALLOY: Yes, sir.

3:35 P.M.

Conversation between
Margaret Narwin and Dr. Gertrude Doane,
Principal, Harrison High

DR. DOANE: Come in, Peg. Come in.

MISS NARWIN: Thank you.

DR. DOANE: Do sit down. Would you like some coffee?

MISS NARWIN: No, thank you.

DR. DOANE: Peg, ever since you sent me that note about funds for that summer teaching workshop, I've been meaning to speak to you.

MISS NARWIN: You're very busy.

54

DR. DOANE: Busy? Good grief. Superintendent Seymour has us writing position papers, speaking to chamber of commerce groups . . . the Rotary club. The upcoming budget vote. He's very nervous about it. And the board election. But that's something else. You don't want to hear about that. Many is the time I wish I were back in the classroom. Though, actually, it was while doing some statistics for this budget vote business that I was able to pull something together that's interesting.

MISS NARWIN: Yes?

DR. DOANE: You know how, in your memo, you spoke of going to that workshop—that some of the instructors were—what?—"master teachers."

MISS NARWIN: Yes.

DR. DOANE: Wish we had that program here. The point is, Peg, you are the one who should be a master teacher.

MISS NARWIN: Thank you, but . . .

DR. DOANE: I mean, what I came up with is this. . . . There is a direct statistical tie-in—that is, those students who have taken an English class with you, Peg, score higher on the Iowa tests, the Stanfords, and the SAT verbals.

MISS NARWIN: Is that right?

DR. DOANE: No question. I could show you the figures.

MISS NARWIN: Well, that's nice to know.

DR. DOANE: I felt so bad about not being able to give you that funding. But, Peg, if the truth be known . . . you don't need it. You—the facts are there for all to see— you are our best English teacher. I didn't have to be told that. But there's the truth for the rest of the world to see.

MISS NARWIN: Thank you, Gert. I really appreciate that. I really do.

Conversation
between Philip Malloy's Parents

MRS. MALLOY: Hi, honey.

MR. MALLOY: 'Lo.

MRS. MALLOY: What's the matter? Something wrong?

MR. MALLOY: Got chewed out by Dexter.

MRS. MALLOY: What for?

MR. MALLOY: Some job estimate that went wrong. Wasn't even anything I did.

MRS. MALLOY: I hope you stood up for yourself.

MR. MALLOY: Are you kidding?

MRS. MALLOY: But, honey, if you were right . . .

MR. MALLOY: And get myself in his bad books.

MRS. MALLOY: You wouldn't get yourself—

MR. MALLOY: Susan, please don't bug me about it. I know when to keep my mouth shut.

MRS. MALLOY: But—

MR. MALLOY: You don't understand. I'm sorry I mentioned it. Look, I'm just not in a position of power there. Okay? Just forget it, okay? Just forget it. It's no big thing.

MRS. MALLOY: Sorry I asked.

Discussion
between Philip Malloy and His Parents
During Dinner

PHILIP MALLOY: It happened again.

MRS. MALLOY: What happened?

PHILIP MALLOY: In school. This morning. I was singing "The Star-Spangled Banner." The teacher kicked me out.

MR. MALLOY: You kidding?

PHILIP MALLOY: No, it's true.

MRS. MALLOY: Sent you out of the classroom?

PHILIP MALLOY: To the assistant principal's office.

MR. MALLOY: I hope you stood up for yourself.

PHILIP MALLOY: I spoke to Palleni.

MR. MALLOY: Who?

PHILIP MALLOY: Assistant principal.

MR. MALLOY: What did he say?

PHILIP MALLOY: Sided with Narwin.

MR. MALLOY: Phil, listen to me. Don't give in to that crap. Don't let them push you around. Singing the . . . There must be some mistake.

PHILIP MALLOY: That's the way she is.

MR. MALLOY: You have to stick up for yourself. That's all there is to it. Phil, do what you feel is right. We'll stand behind you.

MRS. MALLOY: It's so hard to believe.

PHILIP MALLOY: She's really nuts.

MR. MALLOY: Must be.

57

9:45 P.M.

From a Letter Written by Margaret Narwin
to Her Sister, Anita Wigham

. . . So you see, Anita, it was gratifying to hear Gertrude talk this way to me, exactly the kind of support teachers need. Certainly it's what I need at this time. I can't tell you how much. It bucks me up.

Many teachers have almost nothing good to say about their administrators, complaining that they fail to support them, much less grasp the complexities of the classroom situation, or that they show only slight concern about their problems. My principal is different.

I'm lucky. . . .

11:05 P.M.

From the Diary of Philip Malloy

Lots of kids bad-mouth their parents, say they never stick up for them or understand them. Or pay any attention to them. Stuff like that. My parents are different.

I'm lucky.

12

Friday, March 30

8:05 A.M.

Discussion
in Margaret Narwin's Homeroom Class

INTERCOM VOICE OF DR. GERTRUDE DOANE, HARRISON HIGH
PRINCIPAL: Good morning to all students, faculty, and
staff. Today is Friday, March 30. Today will be a Schedule
B day.

Today in history: in 1746 on this date was the birth
of Francisco José de Goya. In 1853 on this date Vincent
van Gogh was born. In 1981, on this date, was the at-
tempted assassination of President Ronald Reagan.

Please all rise and stand at respectful, silent attention
for the playing of our national anthem.

Oh, say, can you see by the dawn's early light . . .

MISS NARWIN: Philip, is that you singing again?

What so proudly we hailed at the twilight's last gleaming?
Whose broad stripes and bright stars, thro' the perilous fight . . .

MISS NARWIN: Philip! I am talking to you!

PHILIP MALLOY: I have the right to do it.

O'er the ramparts we watched were so gallantly streaming?
And the rockets' red glare, the bombs bursting in air . . .

MISS NARWIN: The what?

PHILIP MALLOY: The right.

59

Gave proof thro' the night that our flag was still there. . . .

MISS NARWIN: I want you to stop it immediately. Your ac-
tions are thoroughly disrespectful.

PHILIP MALLOY: It's you who's being disrespectful!

Oh, say does that star-spangled banner yet wave . . .

MISS NARWIN: Philip!

O'er the land of the free and the home of the brave?

PHILIP MALLOY: I was being patriotic. That's all. It's a free country. You have no right to stop me. I was just singing to myself.

MISS NARWIN: Philip Malloy, you will leave this room immediately! Report to the principal's office.

PHILIP MALLOY: You can't keep me from being patriotic.

MISS NARWIN: Leave!

PHILIP MALLOY: I'm going. I'm going.

8:42 A.M.

Conversation between Philip Malloy
and Dr. Joseph Palleni, Assistant Principal,
Harrison High

DR. PALLENI: Okay, Philip, you can come into the office. Go on, sit down. Didn't I just see you yesterday?

PHILIP MALLOY: Yeah.

DR. PALLENI: Something with you and Miss Narwin?

60 ■ PHILIP MALLOY: Yeah.

DR. PALLENI: What's happened now?

PHILIP MALLOY: Nothing.

DR. PALLENI: Come on, Phil. Of course it's something. It may be unimportant. Or important. But it's *something*.

Come on, look up at me. You can talk. Now, what's happening? What's going on?

PHILIP MALLOY: Miss Narwin . . .

DR. PALLENI: Go on.

PHILIP MALLOY: She won't let me sing "The Star-Spangled Banner."

DR. PALLENI: Isn't this what we were talking about the last time?

PHILIP MALLOY: She's against me being patriotic.

DR. PALLENI: I thought we agreed that when we have rules in schools, we stick with them. Didn't we agree to that?

PHILIP MALLOY: How can she keep me from singing the national anthem?

DR. PALLENI: Philip . . .

PHILIP MALLOY: Get me out of her classes.

DR. PALLENI: Look, Philip, what do you want me to do? Change the rules just for you? Do you?

PHILIP MALLOY: No, but . . .

DR. PALLENI: I had a real fistfight out there. Todd Becker. Arnie Licber? You know them?

PHILIP MALLOY: Sort of.

DR. PALLENI: Serious fight. Todd took a licking. Ugly. Now, you come in here . . . Look, I'll be straight with you. This is your second time this week. Talk about rules, you're talking suspension. What do you say, Phil, you get up, go back there, and apologize? To Miss Narwin. Say you'll follow rules. Then, as far as I'm concerned, we forget it. Nothing on your record. What do you say? 61

PHILIP MALLOY: I was just singing. . . .

DR. PALLENI: Did you hear me?

PHILIP MALLOY: She's wrong. That's all. She's wrong. No way I'm apologizing.

DR. PALLENI: That's all you have to say?

PHILIP MALLOY: It's a free country.

DR. PALLENI: Nothing is free.

PHILIP MALLOY: Get me out of her classes.

DR. PALLENI: Phil, go sit out there for a while. Cool off. If you want to change your mind about this, tell Miss Mack out front you want to see me again. Otherwise—just so you understand—I check with Miss Narwin, and if she confirms what you said—that you were breaking rules— hey, I call your folks, they come get you—boom!—two- day suspension. Get it? Automatic.

PHILIP MALLOY: But she's wrong.

DR. PALLENI: Philip, I'll level with you. You're the one who is wrong. You're here to get an education. Rules are rules. Now clear out. I've got important business here. Go on. Speak to Miss Mack out there if you change your mind.

PHILIP MALLOY: I'm not going to change my mind. We don't get along. Get me out of her classes.

DR. PALLENI: Philip, out!

9:30 A.M.

Conversation
between Dr. Joseph Palleni
and Margaret Narwin

DR. PALLENI: Excuse me, Miss Narwin, may I have a word with you?

MISS NARWIN: Class, just continue on with reading that scene. I'll be right outside.

DR. PALLENI: Sorry to bother you, Peg. Look, it's about this Phil Malloy.

MISS NARWIN: Something is certainly bothering that boy.

DR. PALLENI: Singing when you asked him not to.

MISS NARWIN: Quite provocative. Trying to create an incident.

DR. PALLENI: Any idea what it's about?

MISS NARWIN: No.

DR. PALLENI: I offered to get him out of this business by coming back and apologizing, but he won't. Two-day suspension.

MISS NARWIN: Maybe it would be better to switch him into another homeroom.

DR. PALLENI: That's what he suggested. And out of your English class too.

MISS NARWIN: He's been doing poorly there.

DR. PALLENI: Maybe that's it.

MISS NARWIN: I think he's lazy.

DR. PALLENI: Let's start with a homeroom change.

MISS NARWIN: He seems to get on with Bernie Lunser.

DR. PALLENI: Good idea.

MISS NARWIN: Suspension might be counterproductive.

DR. PALLENI: I hear you. Won't keep you. The parents might want to talk to you.

MISS NARWIN: I understand. I wish I could reach him. I just don't seem to. Really, a nice boy.

DR. PALLENI: Yeah. Good kid. Maybe something going on at home. Or hormones. Have a girlfriend?

63

MISS NARWIN: Joe, I wouldn't know.

DR. PALLENI: Okay, Peg. Sorry to bother you.

MISS NARWIN: Let me know if I can be of further help.

DR. PALLENI: Catch you later.

Conversation
between Philip Malloy
and Dr. Joseph Palleni

DR. PALLENI: Now, Philip, I checked with Miss Narwin, and she is in agreement with you. You did break the rules. She also made a point of saying she was prepared to let bygones be bygones if you do as I suggested, apologize and promise not to do that again.

PHILIP MALLOY: No.

DR. PALLENI: Hey, come on, Phil, it'll be a shame to put something down on your record. It's a perfectly good one.

PHILIP MALLOY: No.

DR. PALLENI: Then, Phil, I'm prepared to call one of your parents to come get you and take you home. You'll be out for the rest of the day and . . . I could make it Monday and Tuesday, but . . . How about just Monday? Give you a long weekend to think it out.

PHILIP MALLOY: I'm not going to change my mind.

DR. PALLENI: Okay, who do you want me to call? Your mother or your father?

PHILIP MALLOY: My father doesn't like to be called at work.

DR. PALLENI: Too bad. Is your mother reachable? I can't read a shrug.

64

PHILIP MALLOY: She works too.

DR. PALLENI: Where?

PHILIP MALLOY: At the phone company.

DR. PALLENI: I guess we can reach her. I'll call her. Last chance, Phil.

PHILIP MALLOY: Can't you just change—

DR. PALLENI: First things first. An apology.

PHILIP MALLOY: Call her.

9:59 A.M.

Phone Conversation
between Dr. Joseph Palleni
and Mrs. Malloy

DR. PALLENI: Hello? Is this Mrs. Malloy? Phil's mother?

MRS. MALLOY: Yes, it is.

DR. PALLENI: This is Dr. Palleni, assistant principal at Harrison High.

MRS. MALLOY: Is something the matter with Philip?

DR. PALLENI: Well, no, not exactly. He's sitting right here in front of me. In perfect health. Mrs. Malloy, I'm afraid we've had a little incident here—rule-breaking.

MRS. MALLOY: What happened?

DR. PALLENI: And breaking a rule twice in one week after he'd been warned once.

MRS. MALLOY: What rule?

DR. PALLENI: In fact, Philip was offered—I just offered it— a chance to apologize to the teacher in question, but he won't take it. So, I'm afraid—let me stress this is Phil's decision, not mine—what we have here is a two-day suspension situation. I'm afraid you'll have to come and take him home.

MRS. MALLOY: Now?

DR. PALLENI: Yes, now.

MRS. MALLOY: I'm at my job.

DR. PALLENI: I am sorry. You will have to come.

MRS. MALLOY: What rule did he break?

DR. PALLENI: We can talk about it when you get here. I'd rather we all—you, me, and Philip—talk about it together.

MRS. MALLOY: I have to get permission.

DR. PALLENI: I understand.

MRS. MALLOY: I'll come over.

DR. PALLENI: Thank you.

10:04 A.M.

Conversation
between Philip Malloy
and Dr. Joseph Palleni

PHILIP MALLOY: She coming?

DR. PALLENI: Did you think she wouldn't? Philip, you're bringing a bunch of grief to yourself. And a bother to her. Now, last chance—apologize?

PHILIP MALLOY: No.

DR. PALLENI: Go wait out there until your mother comes.

Phone Conversation
between Philip Malloy's Parents

MR. MALLOY: Susan, I wish you wouldn't call me like this. It's very tense around here today.

MRS. MALLOY: I had to speak to you. I just got a call from Phil's school.

MR. MALLOY: Something the matter? What's up?

MRS. MALLOY: They're going to suspend him.

MR. MALLOY: Phil?

MRS. MALLOY: It was the principal. I have to go in and get him. He's suspended.

MR. MALLOY: Why?

MRS. MALLOY: Some rule.

MR. MALLOY: What rule? Didn't you ask?

MRS. MALLOY: They wouldn't tell me.

MR. MALLOY: They can't just . . .

MRS. MALLOY: I'm really upset.

MR. MALLOY: What it is, is they're really after the kid.

MRS. MALLOY: I don't know. . . .

MR. MALLOY: I'm going to give them a piece of my mind.

MRS. MALLOY: Don't you think we should—

MR. MALLOY: Susan, the kid has done nothing!

MRS. MALLOY: We can speak—

MR. MALLOY: Honey, I have to go. Something just came up.

67
■

MEMO

HARRISON SCHOOL DISTRICT

Where Our Children Are Educated, Not Just Taught

Dr. Albert Seymour
Superintendent

Mrs. Gloria Harland
Chairman, School Board

TO: PHILIP MALLOY
FROM: DR. JOSEPH PALLENI,
    ASSISTANT PRINCIPAL,
    HARRISON HIGH SCHOOL
RE: NEW HOMEROOM ASSIGNMENTS
    FOR SPRING TERM

Dear <u> Philip </u>,

    As we head into the Spring term, the faculty committee has made some changes in homeroom assignments. This will facilitate the movements of students, as well as allow for a greater degree of freedom in the planning of Spring term extracurricular schedules.
    Your new homeroom teacher is: <u> Mr. Lunser </u>, in room: <u> 304 </u>. Effective <u> Tuesday, April 3,</u> <u>8 A.M. </u>
    Thank you for your cooperation.

DR. JOSEPH PALLENI
Assistant Principal

Conversation
among Philip Malloy, Mrs. Malloy,
and Dr. Joseph Palleni

DR. PALLENI: Okay, this is what we've got here. Philip broke a rule. Twice. He and I talked it over earlier this week. I made it clear what would happen. We try to be flexible, but we still have rules. Everybody has to work together. Cooperation. If a student creates a disturbance in a classroom, that's breaking a rule. An important rule. Students cannot break—cannot make a disturbance in a classroom. Straightforward rule infraction. Now, we offered Philip here a chance—he has a perfectly clean record—an opportunity to apologize to the teacher in question. I'll offer it again. Will you do that, Phil, apologize, so we can just end all this?

PHILIP MALLOY: She really dislikes me.

DR. PALLENI: Who is that?

PHILIP MALLOY: Narwin.

MRS. MALLOY: Philip has been saying that—

DR. PALLENI: Look, Mrs. Malloy, I don't want to get into that. Philip admits he broke a rule.

MRS. MALLOY: What rule?

DR. PALLENI: Disturbing a class.

PHILIP MALLOY: Singing the national anthem.

MRS. MALLOY: Is that the rule?

DR. PALLENI: Yes, disturbing the class.

MRS. MALLOY: I just can't believe that—

DR. PALLENI: Excuse me. Philip, did you break the rule?

69

PHILIP MALLOY: It's a dumb rule.

DR. PALLENI: See? He's admitting it. Mrs. Malloy, it is my job—one of my jobs—to make sure the school—the kids, the staff, the teachers—works together in harmony. I'm sure we agree that we can't have kids deciding which rules to follow and which rules not to follow. I really don't wish to discuss it. Two-day suspension. For the rest of today. And Monday. Be back on Tuesday.

MRS. MALLOY: I just want to say I don't think it's right. I mean, singing the—

DR. PALLENI: Excuse me. Are you saying that kids should only follow the rules they want to?

MRS. MALLOY: No, but—

DR. PALLENI: Then we're in agreement. Thank you for coming in. Philip, I hope you think about it.

11:02 A. M.

Conversation
between Philip Malloy and His Mother
on Their Way Home

MRS. MALLOY: Phil, what *is* this all about?

PHILIP MALLOY: I told you, that teacher . . .

MRS. MALLOY: You've never been suspended.

PHILIP MALLOY: It's her.

70

MRS. MALLOY: But why?

PHILIP MALLOY: I don't know.

MRS. MALLOY: They said you could apologize.

PHILIP MALLOY: Nothing to apologize about.

MRS. MALLOY: Your father is going to be very upset.

PHILIP MALLOY: Yeah, well, he told me I should stick up for myself. Said I shouldn't let her push me around. That she was wrong and I was right. So I did.

MRS. MALLOY: When did he say that?

PHILIP MALLOY: Last night. Said I should do what was right.

MRS. MALLOY: Mr.—What's his name?

PHILIP MALLOY: Palleni.

MRS. MALLOY: —said you were creating a disturbance.

PHILIP MALLOY: Bull. It's all her fault.

MRS. MALLOY: Who?

PHILIP MALLOY: Narwin!

MRS. MALLOY: We'll talk it out with your father when he gets home tonight.

PHILIP MALLOY: No way I'm going back to her class again.

MRS. MALLOY: Sometimes I think we should have sent you to Washington Academy.

PHILIP MALLOY: Geeky private school? No way.

MRS. MALLOY: We'll talk. I just want you to know I'm very upset.

PHILIP MALLOY: Sorry.

MEMO

HARRISON SCHOOL DISTRICT

Where Our Children Are Educated, Not Just Taught

Dr. Albert Seymour
Superintendent

Mrs. Gloria Harland
Chairman, School Board

TO: MARGARET NARWIN
FROM: DR. JOSEPH PALLENI,
      ASSISTANT PRINCIPAL,
      HARRISON HIGH SCHOOL
RE: PHILIP MALLOY

Philip Malloy has been suspended for two days—effective today—for causing a disturbance in your homeroom class. I also transferred him back to Mr. Lunser for homeroom.

MEMO

HARRISON SCHOOL DISTRICT

Where Our Children Are Educated, Not Just Taught

Dr. Albert Seymour
Superintendent

Mrs. Gloria Harland
Chairman, School Board

TO: BERNARD LUNSER
FROM: DR. JOSEPH PALLENI,
      ASSISTANT PRINCIPAL,
      HARRISON HIGH SCHOOL
RE: PHILIP MALLOY

Philip Malloy will be returning to you as his home-room teacher effective April 3. He has been suspended for two days— effective today—for causing a disturbance in Miss Narwin's class. While what is involved here is only a minor infraction, more acting out than anything else, there may be some personal problems with the boy (at home?), so I would appreciate hearing from you as to Philip's behavior in your class. I should like to be helpful to him.

MEMO

HARRISON SCHOOL DISTRICT

Where Our Children Are Educated, Not Just Taught

Dr. Albert Seymour
Superintendent

Mrs. Gloria Harland
Chairman, School Board

TO: DR. GERTRUDE DOANE, PRINCIPAL
FROM: DR. JOSEPH PALLENI,
       ASSISTANT PRINCIPAL,
       HARRISON HIGH SCHOOL
RE: PHILIP MALLOY

   Philip Malloy (ninth grade) has been suspended for two days—effective today—for causing a disturbance in Miss Narwin's homeroom class. Because I feel that the problem may have arisen out of some obscure tension between teacher and student, I decided it was advisable to transfer the boy to Mr. Lunser's homeroom.

   Since I assume nothing more will come of this, I'm not aware of anything here that requires your further attention.

12:46 P.M.

Conversation
between Margaret Narwin
and Dr. Joseph Palleni

DR. PALLENI: Oh, Peg! I know you're rushing off. Look, just want you to know I took care of the Malloy boy. Talked

to his mother. She understands. Couple of days' suspension. No big deal.

MISS NARWIN: Did you have to suspend him?

DR. PALLENI: The rule. Two infractions in one week. Anyway, I put a memo in your box. Also, switched him back
to Bernie for homeroom. What about his English class?

MISS NARWIN: I don't want to give up on him yet.

DR. PALLENI: Whatever you say.

MISS NARWIN: He's really a nice boy. Thanks for taking care
of it.

DR. PALLENI: No problem.

MISS NARWIN: I have a class. . . .

DR. PALLENI: Have a good one.

3:45 P.M.

Phone Conversation
between Philip Malloy and Ken Barchet

KEN BARCHET: Hey, Phil, what's happening?

PHILIP MALLOY: Nothing. Going out to deliver my papers.

KEN BARCHET: I heard you got suspended.

PHILIP MALLOY: Yeah.

KEN BARCHET: For how long?

PHILIP MALLOY: Couple of days.

KEN BARCHET: What for?

PHILIP MALLOY: You were there.

KEN BARCHET: Because of your singing?

PHILIP MALLOY: Yeah.

KEN BARCHET: I thought that was funny. Too cool.

PHILIP MALLOY: Wasn't loud.

KEN BARCHET: I heard it. She'd like to throw a fit.

PHILIP MALLOY: Yeah.

KEN BARCHET: I mean, far-out. What made you do it?

PHILIP MALLOY: Free country.

KEN BARCHET: Not as if you have a good voice. People were cracking up.

PHILIP MALLOY: I know. Was Allison laughing?

KEN BARCHET: I don't know. We going to work out after your deliveries?

PHILIP MALLOY: Sure.

KEN BARCHET: See you at the park.

3:48 P.M.

Phone Conversation
between Philip Malloy and Allison Doresett

ALLISON DORESETT: Is this Phil?

PHILIP MALLOY: Yeah.

ALLISON DORESETT: This is Allison.

PHILIP MALLOY: Oh, hi.

ALLISON DORESETT: Is it true that you got suspended?

PHILIP MALLOY: Yeah.

ALLISON DORESETT: Why?

PHILIP MALLOY: Nothing. You were there.

ALLISON DORESETT: The singing?

PHILIP MALLOY: Yeah. "The Star-Spangled Banner."

ALLISON DORESETT: That?

PHILIP MALLOY: Yeah. Narwin got me kicked out.

ALLISON DORESETT: You're kidding. She wouldn't do that.

PHILIP MALLOY: She did. You saw it.

ALLISON DORESETT: No, I mean, she's nice.

PHILIP MALLOY: I don't think so.

ALLISON DORESETT: For how long?

PHILIP MALLOY: Two days.

ALLISON DORESETT: Wow. You must have really got on her nerves.

PHILIP MALLOY: Just singing . . . humming.

ALLISON DORESETT: Well, I just wanted to know. People were talking.

PHILIP MALLOY: What were they saying?

ALLISON DORESETT: You know. How weird. See you.

PHILIP MALLOY: See you.

5:30 P.M.

From a Letter Written by Margaret Narwin to Her Sister, Anita Wigham

---

77

. . . So you see, Anita, what intrigues me about this new concept of teaching English—Whole Language—is that it has its focus on *literature*, and in a way that I think young people will find very interesting. Still, I can hear you say, "It's just another education fad."

You may be right. But if the truth be known, Anita, teaching is exhausting. And what I say is this: if it takes a "fad" to pump energy back into the classroom, why, it's worth it just for that!

Sorry to have gone on so long about this. It's just caught my fancy. I can hardly think about anything else.

Oh, yes, do you remember my writing to you about a student I have, Philip Malloy? I'm convinced now that there is something going on in this boy's private life that is deeply troubling to him. Twice this week I had to send him out for being disruptive in a singularly disrespectful way. Our society is always asking schools to do what is not done at home. Then Joe Palleni (assistant principal) felt compelled to suspend him for a bit, something I *never* believe is productive. I told him that too. In fact, Philip is a nice boy. So I do feel badly about the whole thing. I always do when I lose a student. Next week—when he comes back—I intend to sit down with him and have a heart-to-heart talk.

This weekend I'll be visiting with Barbara Benthave. She and her husband . . .

6:45 P.M.

Discussion
between Philip Malloy's Parents

MRS. MALLOY: Oh, hi, honey.

MR. MALLOY: Where's Philip?

MRS. MALLOY: Up in the shower. Just got back from running.

MR. MALLOY: You talk to him about what happened?

MRS. MALLOY: When I drove him home. But I had to get right back to work. It's just what I told you. How was your day?

MR. MALLOY: Rotten. Dexter is still sore at me.

MRS. MALLOY: Get yourself a drink to settle down first. We have plenty of time to talk over dinner.

MR. MALLOY: Sure.

7:12 P.M.

Discussion between Philip Malloy and His Parents During Dinner

---

MR. MALLOY: Okay, Phil. Now, I want to hear the whole thing. Start to finish. Just understand, right from the start, we're on your side. We don't intend to just take it. But I have to know what happened. Go on now.

PHILIP MALLOY: Same as before.

MR. MALLOY: Same as *what* before?

MRS. MALLOY: He's trying to tell you, dear.

PHILIP MALLOY: See, they play "The Star-Spangled Banner" at the beginning of school. . . .

MR. MALLOY: I understand. When I was a kid we pledged allegiance. Go on.

PHILIP MALLOY: A tape.

MR. MALLOY: Okay.

PHILIP MALLOY: When—before—when I was in Mr. Lunser's class, he was like, almost asking me to sing out loud.

MRS. MALLOY: I always thought Philip had a good voice.

MR. MALLOY: That's not exactly relevant! Go on.

PHILIP MALLOY: But this teacher—

79
∎

MR. MALLOY: Mrs. Narwin.

PHILIP MALLOY: It's Miss.

MR. MALLOY: Figures.

MRS. MALLOY: That has nothing to do with it, Ben!

MR. MALLOY: Go on.

PHILIP MALLOY: She won't let me. Threw me out of class.

MRS. MALLOY: The principal said it was a rule.

PHILIP MALLOY: Ma, he's the *assistant* principal.

MR. MALLOY: But why does that mean suspension?

PHILIP MALLOY: She threw me out twice this week.

MR. MALLOY: It seems arbitrary. Outrageous.

MRS. MALLOY: Stupid rules.

MR. MALLOY: Right. How can you have a rule against singing "The Star-Spangled Banner"?

PHILIP MALLOY: Ask Narwin.

MR. MALLOY: You know who I bet would be interested in this?

PHILIP MALLOY: Who?

MR. MALLOY: Ted Griffen.

MRS. MALLOY: Why?

MR. MALLOY: He's a neighbor. A friend. And he's running for school board. He should be interested. That's what the board does. Keeps the schools in line.

PHILIP MALLOY: He won't be able to do anything. If I could just get out of her classes.

MR. MALLOY: Maybe. Maybe not. Phil, we intend to support you on this.

Conversation
among Philip Malloy, Mr. Malloy,
and Ted Griffen

PHILIP MALLOY: Dad, I don't think he'll be interested.

MR. MALLOY: Of course he will. Now, just let me do the talking. Ted! Hello.

MR. GRIFFEN: Oh, Ben. Hello. Is that you, Philip? How you guys doing?

MR. MALLOY: Ted, got a minute? This a bad time?

MR. GRIFFEN: Well, I am in the middle of a talk with—why, what's up?

MR. MALLOY: Something about school. And Phil here. . . .

MR. GRIFFEN: I'm not on the school board yet, Ben. Trying, but not yet.

MR. MALLOY: That's the point. This is something that happened to Phil at school.

MR. GRIFFEN: I don't know if I should . . .

MR. MALLOY: He was suspended for *singing* "The Star-Spangled Banner."

MR. GRIFFEN: What?

MR. MALLOY: You heard me. Phil was kicked out of school for singing "The Star-Spangled Banner."

MR. GRIFFEN: Are you serious?

MR. MALLOY: I know. It's crazy. Today.

MR. GRIFFEN: That true?

PHILIP MALLOY: Yes, sir.

MR. GRIFFEN: Singing?

81
■

MR. MALLOY: We couldn't believe it at first either. But they called Susan at work, mind you. Made her leave work and bring him home. Two-day suspension. For *singing*.

MR. GRIFFEN: Who did it?

MR. MALLOY: The principal.

PHILIP MALLOY: Assistant principal.

MR. GRIFFEN: When were you singing?

MR. MALLOY: Tell him.

PHILIP MALLOY: They sing, play the . . . the national anthem in the morning. And I, like—I was singing it. Mostly to myself. Then, I have this teacher—people don't like her—and she, well, she threw me out of the class and—

MR. GRIFFEN: Wait a minute. I want to get this straight. Look, I have this reporter I'm talking to. Jennifer Stewart. From the *Manchester Record*. School beat. How about talking to me with her there?

MR. MALLOY: What do you say?

PHILIP MALLOY: A reporter?

MR. GRIFFEN: She does their educational stuff. She's covering school board elections around the state. A good person.

PHILIP MALLOY: I don't know. . . .

MR. GRIFFEN: Nothing to worry about. Very straightforward. I'd like her to hear about this. Really, I would. Just tell her the truth. You don't mind, do you, Ben?

MR. MALLOY: No.

82

MR. GRIFFEN: Phil?

PHILIP MALLOY: Well . . .

MR. GRIFFEN: Sure. Just tell her the truth. Come on in.

Conversation among
Philip Malloy, Mr. Malloy, Ted Griffen,
and Jennifer Stewart, Education Reporter
from the *Manchester Record*

MR. GRIFFEN: Jennifer, this is my neighbor from across the street, Ben Malloy. His son, Phil Malloy. Jennifer Stewart, from the *Manchester Record*.

MS. STEWART: Pleased to meet you.

MR. MALLOY: Evening.

MR. GRIFFEN: Jennifer was just interviewing me for a piece she's doing on the school board elections. Statewide. These guys think I'm such a shoo-in to be elected they're already bringing me problems.

MS. STEWART: Shows a lot of confidence in you.

MR. GRIFFEN: Actually, people are tired of the old ways. Not happy with the way things are. Now, for example, this thing, these guys, Phil here, tells me something that's outrageous. Something I would never condone.

MS. STEWART: What's that?

MR. MALLOY: Phil, tell her what you told Ted.

MS. STEWART: This something . . . Is it Philip?

MR. MALLOY: Yes. Philip. M–a–l–l–o–y.

MS. STEWART: This something that happened to you?

MR. GRIFFEN: He lives right across the street. Neighbors. Old—and good—friends.

MR. MALLOY: Phil, tell her what happened. Exactly as it was. This was just today.

MS. STEWART: Philip?

PHILIP MALLOY: Well, see, there's this teacher.

MR. MALLOY: Go on.

PHILIP MALLOY: Miss Narwin, English teacher, and she doesn't like me. . . .

MR. GRIFFEN: No. Tell her what you told me.

MR. MALLOY: This is part of it.

MS. STEWART: Tell it your own way, Philip.

PHILIP MALLOY: In the mornings, at school, in homeroom, before morning announcements, they play "The Star-Spangled Banner."

MS. STEWART: Who plays?

PHILIP MALLOY: The school. On the sound system.

MS. STEWART: Just want to get this down. Okay. Go on.

PHILIP MALLOY: And, I like to sing along.

MR. MALLOY: It's the way we've brought him up.

MR. GRIFFEN: The whole neighborhood is like that.

MS. STEWART: Go on, Philip.

PHILIP MALLOY: And this teacher . . .

MS. STEWART: Could you spell her name?

PHILIP MALLOY: Miss Narwin.

MR. MALLOY: M–a–r–w–i–n. She's always on the boy's back. Bad teacher. The kids don't like her.

MR. GRIFFEN: Narwin? Or Marwin?

MR. MALLOY: Right.

MS. STEWART: Go on, Philip.

PHILIP MALLOY: Well, I like to, you know, sing along. But, see, she kicked me out. For singing it.

MS. STEWART: The national anthem?

MR. GRIFFEN: Hard to believe.

MR. MALLOY: It's true. The principal even admitted it to my wife.

PHILIP MALLOY: Assistant principal.

MR. MALLOY: Well, anyway, they admit it.

MS. STEWART: Is there more?

PHILIP MALLOY: It happened again.

MS. STEWART: Twice?

PHILIP MALLOY: Yeah. Three times, actually.

MS. STEWART: And?

PHILIP MALLOY: They suspended me.

MR. GRIFFEN: How anyone could get kicked out of school for . . .

MR. MALLOY: Being patriotic.

MR. GRIFFEN: If I were on the board, I wouldn't accept this. I would not condone this. No way.

MS. STEWART: Philip, was anyone else kicked out?

PHILIP MALLOY: Just me.

MS. STEWART: Do you have any sense as to why you in particular?

PHILIP MALLOY: They have a rule against it.

MS. STEWART: Rule against what?

MR. MALLOY: Singing "The Star-Spangled Banner."

MR. GRIFFEN: Absurd!

MS. STEWART: And this is something I can check out?   85

PHILIP MALLOY: I guess. Sure. Go on.

MR. MALLOY: The principal admitted it.

MR. GRIFFEN: Jennifer, and you can quote me on this, I

don't intend to be silent about this issue. This is a school, an American school, and parents have a right to expect that certain things, like values, will be taught. Community values. Things I believe in. I mean that. Sincerely.

11:34 P.M.

From the Diary of Philip Malloy

It really hit the fan today. So much happened I have a headache. It's going to take a while to think out. Actually, I don't feel so great. In a way, the whole thing is stupid. But everybody says I was right. And I was.

13

Saturday, March 31

10:00 A.M.

Phone Conversation
between Jennifer Stewart
of the *Manchester Record*
and Dr. Albert Seymour,
Harrison School Superintendent

MS. STEWART: May I speak to Dr. Albert Seymour, please.

DR. SEYMOUR: Speaking.

MS. STEWART: Dr. Seymour, this is Jennifer Stewart of the *Manchester Record*.

DR. SEYMOUR: How do you do?

MS. STEWART: I hope you don't mind a call at home. I'm the education reporter.

DR. SEYMOUR: Oh, yes.

MS. STEWART: Something has come up—a report, sir—and I wanted to check some facts with you.

DR. SEYMOUR: If I can be helpful . . . certainly.

MS. STEWART: Sir, does the Harrison School District have a rule that forbids students from singing "The Star-Spangled Banner"?

DR. SEYMOUR: Beg pardon?

MS. STEWART: Yes, sir. Does the Harrison School District have a rule that students are not allowed to sing "The Star-Spangled Banner"?

DR. SEYMOUR: Of course not. Whatever gave you that idea? Who told you that?

87
■

MS. STEWART: There's been a claim . . .

DR. SEYMOUR: Hogwash. You should check your sources.

MS. STEWART: I'm checking them right now.

DR. SEYMOUR: The answer is no. We do not have such a rule. Absolutely.

MS. STEWART: May I quote you?

DR. SEYMOUR: Of course.

MS. STEWART: Thank you.

DR. SEYMOUR: You're quite welcome.

10:15 A.M.

Phone Conversation between Jennifer Stewart of the *Manchester Record* and Dr. Gertrude Doane, Principal, Harrison High

---

MS. STEWART: May I speak to Dr. Doane, please.

DR. DOANE: This is she.

MS. STEWART: Dr. Doane, my name is Jennifer Stewart, of the *Manchester Record*. I do the school stories. Sorry to bother you on a Saturday. . . .

DR. DOANE: Yes?

MS. STEWART: I'm checking out an item that's come to our attention. It would appear that one of your students, Philip Malloy—

DR. DOANE: Ninth grade.

MS. STEWART: You know him?

DR. DOANE: Oh, yes. Nice boy. Know him well. Has something happened to him?

MS. STEWART: This is in reference to his suspension from school.

DR. DOANE: Suspension?

MS. STEWART: Isn't that something— a suspension—that as principal you would know something about?

DR. DOANE: Well, yes. . . .

MS. STEWART: On Friday, March 30, yesterday, Philip Malloy—*he* claims, as his parents claim, that he was suspended from your high school for two days.

DR. DOANE: Discipline problems are usually in the hands of my assistant principal, Dr. Palleni. In any case I was at meetings all—

MS. STEWART: Wouldn't Dr. Palleni discuss such a suspension with you first?

DR. DOANE: That would depend on . . . Ms. . . .

MS. STEWART: Stewart.

DR. DOANE: Ms. Stewart, actually I'm not sure I should be discussing this matter with you. Records regarding our children are of a confidential nature.

MS. STEWART: It's already a matter of public record. The boy—and his father—have made a public statement. They claim he was suspended.

DR. DOANE: That's what you say.

MS. STEWART: Dr. Doane, if you don't wish to cooperate . . .

DR. DOANE: Now just one moment, Ms. . . .

MS. STEWART: Stewart.

DR. DOANE: Ms. Stewart, you call me up and inform me about something of which I have had no prior information. . . .

MS. STEWART: Then you didn't know about this?

DR. DOANE: I just said—

MS. STEWART: Ms. Doane—

DR. DOANE: *Dr.* Doane.

MS. STEWART: Excuse me. Dr. Doane, Philip Malloy, who is a student at your school, and who you claim to know well, has made a statement to the effect that he was suspended for singing "The Star-Spangled Banner."

DR. DOANE: Oh, really!

MS. STEWART: His father claims this is true. Now, I just spoke to your superintendent. . . .

DR. DOANE: Dr. Seymour?

MS. STEWART: That's right. And he says that the Harrison School District has no such rule. So, I am just trying to sort this out. . . .

DR. DOANE: I don't know the particulars of this situation. You've only just informed me about it. I see no reason to be talking to a reporter about a student's problem. In any case, it doesn't seem to have happened. The superintendent told you we have no such rule.

MS. STEWART: Would a student in your school run into difficulty by singing the national anthem?

DR. DOANE: Of course not. But I repeat: discipline problems of a minor nature are handled by my assistant principal.

MS. STEWART: Palleni?

DR. DOANE: That's right. Dr. Joseph Palleni.

MS. STEWART: Thank you.

Discussion
between Philip Malloy and His Mother

PHILIP MALLOY: Hey, Ma, look! Look at this letter.

MRS. MALLOY: What letter?

PHILIP MALLOY: Just came in the mail. Look. They shifted me out of Narwin's homeroom class. Back to Mr. Lunser.

MRS. MALLOY: Let me see. Well, that's something. They must have seen something was wrong there. Maybe you can go back to school Monday.

PHILIP MALLOY: Says it won't happen till Tuesday. When I go back.

MRS. MALLOY: May be just as well. I don't want you to have to deal with that woman again.

PHILIP MALLOY: But I still have her for English.

MRS. MALLOY: Didn't they change that?

PHILIP MALLOY: No.

MRS. MALLOY: But if they admit they're wrong about the one thing . . .

PHILIP MALLOY: Bet they just forgot to say that. Where's Dad?

MRS. MALLOY: Went to the store. Feel better?

PHILIP MALLOY: Yeah. But the English . . .

MRS. MALLOY: You just said they forgot.

PHILIP MALLOY: I guess. . . .

91
■

Phone Conversation
between Jennifer Stewart
of the *Manchester Record*
and Dr. and Mrs. Joseph Palleni

MS. STEWART: May I speak to Dr. Joseph Palleni, please?

MRS. PALLENI: Who's calling, please?

MS. STEWART: Jennifer Stewart, reporter for the *Manchester Record.*

MRS. PALLENI: He's in the backyard. I'll get him.

MS. STEWART: Appreciate that.

DR. PALLENI: Hello? This is Dr. Palleni.

MS. STEWART: Dr. Palleni, this is Jennifer Stewart. I'm a reporter for the *Manchester Record.* I'm doing a story— I've already spoken with your superintendent, Dr. Seymour, and your principal, Dr. Doane—

DR. PALLENI: What is this about?

MS. STEWART: Dr. Palleni, according to Dr. Seymour, the Harrison School District has no rule that would keep a student from singing "The Star-Spangled Banner."

DR. PALLENI: Did you say *singing?*

MS. STEWART: Yes. Is that your understanding?

DR. PALLENI: Well . . .

MS. STEWART: Now your principal, Dr. Doane, says that you are in charge of discipline in the school.

DR. PALLENI: *With* her.

MS. STEWART: With her?

DR. PALLENI: I always keep her informed.

MS. STEWART: Did you inform her that on Friday you suspended a student, Philip Malloy, for singing "The Star-
Spangled Banner"?

DR. PALLENI: I did no such thing!

MS. STEWART: You didn't inform your superior, or you didn't
suspend the boy for singing "The Star-Spangled Banner"?
Which? I am simply trying to get my facts straight. Dr.
Palleni? Are you still there?

DR. PALLENI: I don't wish to talk to you.

MS. STEWART: No comment?

DR. PALLENI: No comment. But you've got your facts all
wrong.

MS. STEWART: Is that your comment?

DR. PALLENI: No comment.

MS. STEWART: I'm sorry. Should I call you back?

DR. PALLENI: Not to talk about this.

MS. STEWART: May I quote you?

DR. PALLENI: Thank you. Good-bye.

11:00 A.M.

Phone Conversation
between Jennifer Stewart
of the *Manchester Record*
and Margaret Narwin

MS. STEWART: Margaret Narwin, please.

MISS NARWIN: Speaking.

MS. STEWART: Miss Narwin, my name is Jennifer Stewart,
of the *Manchester Record.* The education reporter. I'm

trying to write a story regarding an incident—something that appears to have happened in your school, in your class. I understand you are a teacher.

MISS NARWIN: An English teacher. In the high school.

MS. STEWART: How long have you taught there?

MISS NARWIN: For twenty-one years. What incident are you referring to? I'm not aware . . .

MS. STEWART: I'm simply trying to get the facts correct. Wanting to be fair to all concerned. I'm sure you can appreciate that.

MISS NARWIN: Are you sure this has something to do with me?

MS. STEWART: That appears to be the case. And, as I say, I want to be fair to all concerned, and report the facts correctly.

MISS NARWIN: I'm afraid I don't understand. . . .

MS. STEWART: I spoke to your superintendent, your principal, and your assistant principal, as well as Philip Malloy and his father.

MISS NARWIN: Who?

MS. STEWART: Philip Malloy. I believe he is one of your students.

MISS NARWIN: Well . . .

MS. STEWART: Now, as I understand it, the boy was dismissed from your class, then suspended from school because—he says it's a question of patriotism with him—he sang "The Star-Spangled Banner" during opening exercises in school in your class. Could you shed some light on this? Miss Narwin? Are you there?

MISS NARWIN: Yes. . . .

MS. STEWART: Could you give me your side of the story?

MISS NARWIN: The boy was creating a disturbance.

MS. STEWART: I'm sorry. I couldn't hear you. Could you speak up?

MISS NARWIN: The boy was creating a serious disturbance.

MS. STEWART: By singing the national anthem?

MISS NARWIN: We have a rule. . . .

MS. STEWART: Your superintendent, Dr. Seymour, says there is no rule.

MISS NARWIN: I don't think I should be talking about this.

MS. STEWART: But you do acknowledge that you sent him from your room?

MISS NARWIN: Yes, but . . .

MS. STEWART: For singing our national anthem?

MISS NARWIN: I think you need to speak to our principal.

MS. STEWART: I did speak to her.

MISS NARWIN: Then I have nothing more to say.

MS. STEWART: You are sure?

MISS NARWIN: Quite sure.

MS. STEWART: Thank you, Miss . . . or is it *Mrs.* Narwin?

MISS NARWIN: Miss.

MS. STEWART: Thank you.

MISS NARWIN: Thank you.

Phone Conversation
between Dr. Gertrude Doane
and Dr. Joseph Palleni

DR. DOANE: Joe, sorry to bother you at home.

DR. PALLENI: That's all right. . . .

DR. DOANE: I just got a call from a newspaper reporter—
Manchester Record—

DR. PALLENI: Oh, right. She called me.

DR. DOANE: She did?

DR. PALLENI: About a suspension—Philip Malloy. On Friday.

DR. DOANE: What is this? I was at district meetings. What's
this all about? Why should a reporter be calling?

DR. PALLENI: I put a memo in your box. Yesterday.

DR. DOANE: Joe, I was at meetings.

DR. PALLENI: Right. I know. Okay. The Malloy boy was
suspended for two days—actually, less—because he was
causing a disturbance in Peg Narwin's class.

DR. DOANE: Joe, what this reporter said—told me—it was
for *singing* "The Star-Spangled Banner." What's this all
about?

DR. PALLENI: Oh, no, no. Nothing like that. It was just that
he—Philip—was acting out in class. Look, Gert, he did
it twice this week. So I had to suspend him. Look. I, you
know, I talked it over with the kid. He agrees about what
happened. He does. That's not an issue. Besides, I gave
him a chance to work it out, you know, apologize, promise
not to do it again. He's okay. I mean, his record is perfect.

Didn't seem like much of a thing. But he wouldn't swallow his pride. Something else, I suspect. At home. Hormones. You name it. Anyway, that's all it is.

DR. DOANE: But why should a reporter call me?

DR. PALLENI: I don't know. As I said, she called me too.

DR. DOANE: What did you tell her?

DR. PALLENI: Told her to mind her own business.

DR. DOANE: Joe . . .

DR. PALLENI: Good Lord, Gert, if I had to discuss every little problem we have with the kids with every fool reporter . . .

DR. DOANE: I know. I know.

DR. PALLENI: Do you want me to talk to her? Suppose I could track her down.

DR. DOANE: Not if it was only what you said it was.

DR. PALLENI: It was. Believe me. It was.

DR. DOANE: Okay. If she does call back, you can just refer her to me.

DR. PALLENI: Will do.

DR. DOANE: Have a nice weekend, Joe. Sorry to bother you.

DR. PALLENI: No problem. Have a good one, Gert.

11:45 P.M.

From the Diary of Philip Malloy

Aside from getting out of Narwin's homeroom—still not out of her English—not much of anything today. Boring! Newspapers to deliver. Collection day. Can't understand how people who want the paper think they can get away with not paying for it. And it comes out of my pocket. Then folks made me do yard work. Clean up room. Ken came over.

Been trying to figure a way to get on the school track team. Maybe—like the coach said—I should ask Narwin for extra work. Be worth it. I hate working out without a team. . . .

14

Sunday, April 1

Article
from the Community Section of
the *Manchester Record*

SUSPENDED FOR PATRIOTISM
by J. Stewart, Education Reporter

Harrison. While it may appear to be an April Fools' Day joke, tenth grader Philip Malloy of Harrison High School was suspended for singing "The Star-Spangled Banner."

His parents, Susan and Benjamin Malloy of Harrison Township, do not consider themselves super patriots, but they did raise their son to have pride in our country. It was only natural then for Philip to sing along when the national anthem was played on tape during morning exercises. According to Harrison School superintendent Dr. A. Seymour, there is no rule against singing the anthem. Indeed, in every other class Philip did just that. His new homeroom teacher, Ms. Margaret Narwin, however, changed the rules. Every time Philip lifted his voice to sing she threw him out of class, insisting a disturbance was being created.

School principal Dr. Gertrude Doane, who admits that Philip has no previous bad marks on his record, saw the issue only as one of discipline, and referred all questions regarding school policy to Dr. Joseph Palleni, assistant principal. Dr. Palleni, however, refused to be interviewed regarding the incident.

99
■

What will young Malloy—who has his own delivery route for the *Manchester Record*—do during his suspension from school? Philip, who still hopes to make the school track team this spring, said, "Try to keep up with my work, and work out with classmates after school."

Harrison Township will be voting on a new school district budget this spring, along with a new school board.

8:30 A.M.

Phone Conversation
between Dr. Albert Seymour
and Dr. Gertrude Doane

DR. SEYMOUR: Gertrude?

DR. DOANE: This is Gertrude Doane.

DR. SEYMOUR: Gertrude, Al Seymour here. Did you see this morning's paper?

DR. DOANE: Just reading the first section now.

DR. SEYMOUR: Well, look at section D. Community news. Page two. School news.

DR. DOANE: Why?

DR. SEYMOUR: Just do it.

DR. DOANE: Hold on a moment.

DR. SEYMOUR: Did you find it?

DR. DOANE: Yes, and I . . . Oh my!

DR. SEYMOUR: Read it.

DR. DOANE: This is ridiculous!

DR. SEYMOUR: What is this business? I had a call from a reporter yesterday, but . . . Is any of this true?

DR. DOANE: Al, the boy was not suspended because of singing the national anthem. Of course not. He was suspended because he was creating a disturbance. That's according to Joe.

DR. SEYMOUR: Joe?

DR. DOANE: Joe Palleni.

DR. SEYMOUR: A disturbance by singing? Singing "The Star-Spangled Banner"?

DR. DOANE: Yes. Joe handled it.

DR. SEYMOUR: Who is this Narwin woman?

DR. DOANE: An English teacher. She's been on the staff for years. Actually, longest of all, I think. A good teacher.

DR. SEYMOUR: Oh, yes. Think I know her. And that's all there is to it?

DR. DOANE: As far as I know.

DR. SEYMOUR: Let's hope so. I mean . . .

DR. DOANE: Al, no one could take this seriously.

DR. SEYMOUR: I hope not. I hope not. With the budget vote soon . . . and the school board—

DR. DOANE: Do you want me to call the newspaper?

DR. SEYMOUR: Ah . . . no. But if you get any calls you can refer them all to me. To my office. Tomorrow.

DR. DOANE: I will.

DR. SEYMOUR: This is not going to do us any good.

DR. DOANE: No one reads about schools.

DR. SEYMOUR: Let's hope so.

9:20 A.M.

Phone Conversation
between Philip Malloy and Ken Barchet

PHILIP MALLOY: What's happening?

KEN BARCHET: Did you see the paper?

PHILIP MALLOY: I deliver it. I don't have to read it.

KEN BARCHET: Guess what my ma found in it.

PHILIP MALLOY: What?

KEN BARCHET: It's all about you.

PHILIP MALLOY: Sure. April fool.

KEN BARCHET: No. Really. Look at section D. Page two. A riot.

PHILIP MALLOY: Sure.

KEN BARCHET: It ain't true. But it's funny. We working out?

PHILIP MALLOY: Have to visit my grandma at the nursing home.

KEN BARCHET: Make sure they don't lock you up. See you.

PHILIP MALLOY: Catch you later.

KEN BARCHET: Don't forget to look.

PHILIP MALLOY: April fool.

Conversation
between Philip Malloy's Parents

MRS. MALLOY: Look here, Ben. That reporter did put in a story about Philip.

MR. MALLOY: You're kidding! Let me see.

MRS. MALLOY: Here.

MR. MALLOY: I'll be. . . .

MRS. MALLOY: It's got the whole thing.

MR. MALLOY: See, the superintendent says there's no such rule. It *was* just that teacher.

MRS. MALLOY: Doesn't seem right.

MR. MALLOY: She should be fired. Philip upstairs?

MRS. MALLOY: Think so.

MR. MALLOY: Philip! Come on down here and look at this.

PHILIP MALLOY: What?

MRS. MALLOY: This.

MR. MALLOY: See. If you stick up for yourself, you get action. How's that make you feel? Philip? What do you think?

MRS. MALLOY: What's the matter?

PHILIP MALLOY: I don't know.

MRS. MALLOY: It was the teacher. Just as you said.

PHILIP MALLOY: Weird . . .

MR. MALLOY: Just shows you—

MRS. MALLOY: Where are you going?

PHILIP MALLOY: Upstairs.

103

MRS. MALLOY: We're leaving in half an hour.

MR. MALLOY: Sometimes you just have to deal with things.

MRS. MALLOY: He looked like he was reading his own funeral notice.

MR. MALLOY: Kids . . .

MRS. MALLOY: Well, anyway, you were right. Now maybe the boy can go back to school on Monday. Isn't it odd to see your name in the paper?

MR. MALLOY: I sort of like it. Good if Dexter sees it.

MRS. MALLOY: That Ted Griffen. He knows how to get things done.

MR. MALLOY: Got my vote.

2:30 P.M.

Phone Conversation
between Margaret Narwin and Her Sister,
Anita Wigham

MARGARET NARWIN: I just don't understand why they would ever print such a thing.

ANITA WIGHAM: That's the papers. . . .

MARGARET NARWIN: It's so slanted.

ANITA WIGHAM: Peg, I don't think anybody will pay much attention to it. Just tell people the truth. Put your faith in that.

104

MARGARET NARWIN: I suppose you're right. It's just . . .

ANITA WIGHAM: It will pass.

7:30 P.M.

From a Speech Delivered by Ted Griffen
to a Meeting of the Harrison
Sunday Fellowship

MR. GRIFFEN: . . . so what I will try to do—if elected as a member of the Harrison School Board—is not just keep the cost of education down to a reasonable level—keeping our taxes down—I will work with the rest of the board to support basic American values. For I—and I can only speak for myself—I am shocked that a Harrison student should be suspended from one of our schools because he desires to sing the national anthem. Yes, my friends, it is true. It has happened here. Here—in today's *Record*—is the sad story. And I say, what is the point of installing computers—which my generation never seemed to need—and at great cost—if our young people are not allowed to practice the elemental values of American patriotism?

11:20 P.M.

From the Diary of Philip Malloy

Folks excited—mostly Dad—by a newspaper story about what happened in school. Wonder what will happen now. Dad keeps telling me how great I am.

Maybe they'll kick Miss Narwin out. Wonder if she even saw it. It's her fault. Not mine.

No one called. I guess I don't go to school tomorrow.

Watched some track on TV. Steve Hallick lost a race. Said he wasn't ready. Can't believe it.

Finished *The Outsiders*. Not bad. Wonder what it would be like to live without parents. You could do what you'd like.

105

15

Monday, April 2

From American Affiliated Press
Wire Service

KICKED OUT OF SCHOOL
FOR PATRIOTISM

Harrison, NH. A tenth grader was suspended from his local school because he sang
"The Star-Spangled Banner" during the
school's morning exercises. The boy, Philip
Malloy, who wished to sing in the spirit of
patriotism, was then forced to remain home
alone, since both his parents work. English
teacher Margaret Narwin, who brought about
the suspension, maintains the boy was making a nuisance of himself.

8:05 A.M.

Transcript
from the Jake Barlow Talk Show

JAKE BARLOW: Okay. Okay. Here we go! All sorts of things
we can talk about. Wanting—and waiting—to hear from
you on WLRB, your talk radio with your loudmouthed
host Jake Barlow ready to take you on. Ready. Willing.
And able! All kinds of things going on. We can talk about
that demonstration in Washington. I don't know about
that. I don't know. Bunch of . . . Hey, what do you think
about that point-shaving scandal over at that university

in the Midwest? Come on, guys, is that an education or what? Then there's the president, who's said he would *be* an education president. But he's got his work cut out for him. I'm telling you because here's a bit of a story, bit of a story, that came in over the wires. Don't know if you saw this. Let me read it to you. Now, listen up! This is America. I mean it! WLRB asking you—Jake Barlow asking you—what you think of *this*. Now, remember, I'm not making this up. None of it. I'm *reading* it!

"KICKED OUT OF SCHOOL FOR PATRIOTISM."

Right. You heard me correct. "KICKED OUT OF SCHOOL FOR PATRIOTISM." But you ain't heard nothing yet. Listen to this!

"Harrison, New Hampshire."

Where in the *world* is Harrison? In the United States? In America? Listen up, New Hampshire. All their auto plates read "Live free or die." Well, something died, because this is what is going on there right now! Here it is. The whole story. Right in the morning news. I'm just quoting.

"A tenth grader was suspended from his local school because he sang 'The Star-Spangled Banner' during the school's morning exercises. The boy, Philip Malloy, who wished to sing in the spirit of patriotism, was then forced to remain home alone, since both his parents work. English teacher Margaret Narwin, who brought about the suspension, maintains the boy was making a nuisance of himself."

Would you believe it? Would you believe it. Okay, this is WLRB, all-talk radio. Take a short break, then come right back to talk about whatever you want. Man, but I'm telling you: what's happening to this country!

Now this. . . .

Phone Conversation between
Mrs. Gloria Harland, Chairman,
Harrison School Board, and Dr. Albert Seymour,
Superintendent of Schools

MRS. HARLAND: Albert, this is Gloria Harland. Good morning.

DR. SEYMOUR: Gloria! Good morning. Looks like spring is here.

MRS. HARLAND: It is balmy, isn't it? Albert, last night I attended a meeting of the Harrison Sunday Fellowship. . . .

DR. SEYMOUR: Oh, yes. Couldn't make it.

MRS. HARLAND: Well, Ted Griffen made a speech.

DR. SEYMOUR: Ted Griffen?

MRS. HARLAND: He's running for the school board.

DR. SEYMOUR: Oh, yes. Right. They're doing a series of talks. Know him. Know him well. Bit hard and—

MRS. HARLAND: Albert, part of Ted's speech was an attack on the present board in regard to what he claims is the suspension of a student for singing the national anthem in one of the schools. High school, I think.

DR. SEYMOUR: The what?

MRS. HARLAND: Suspension for singing the national anthem. "The Star-Spangled Banner." And—to my shock—I checked and sure enough, as he said, I saw something about it in the paper yesterday. The Sunday paper. What *is* this all about? We have the vote . . .

DR. SEYMOUR: Oh, Lord, is he going to make a thing about this?

MRS. HARLAND: What happened? It's not true, is it?

DR. SEYMOUR: Gloria, I can assure you nothing of the kind occurred. Nothing. But before I go off half-cocked, let me make some further inquiries and then get back to you.

MRS. HARLAND: Soon.

DR. SEYMOUR: Absolutely. Soon.

MRS. HARLAND: Al, this is *not* what we need. Not with the budget vote so—

DR. SEYMOUR: Exactly. I understand.

8:10 A.M.

Transcript
from the Jake Barlow Talk Show

JAKE BARLOW: Okay. Okay. Back again. And ready to take you on. We've got the scandal out at the U. The demonstration in D.C. The kid kicked out of school for being an American patriot. Anything you want. Here we go. First call. Hello?

CALLER: Is this Jake?

JAKE BARLOW: Jake Cruising-for-a-Bruising Barlow. Who's this?

CALLER: This is Steve.

JAKE BARLOW: Steve! How you doing, big guy?

STEVE: Great. Really like your show. You're doing great.

JAKE BARLOW: Don't tell me! Tell the president of the station, Steve.

STEVE: Yeah. Ha-ha! Right. Look—about that kid.

JAKE BARLOW: The one kicked out of school for singing "The Star-Spangled Banner"?

STEVE: Yeah. Hey, you know, that gripes me. Really does. Things may be different. But, come off it!

JAKE BARLOW: Right! What are schools for, anyway?

STEVE: People might call me a—a—

JAKE BARLOW: Jerk?

STEVE: Yeah, maybe. But like they used to say, America, love it or leave it. And that school—

JAKE BARLOW: It was a teacher.

STEVE: Yeah, teacher. She shouldn't be allowed to teach. That's my opinion.

JAKE BARLOW: Right. I'm right with you there, Steve. I mean, there are the three R's—reading, 'riting, and 'rithmetic—and the three P's—prayer, patriotism, and parents. At least, that's my notion of schooling.

STEVE: Right. I'm right with you.

JAKE BARLOW: Okay, Steve. Like what you said. Let's see if we got any ultraliberals out there who'll call in and try to defend this—I was about to say *woman*—person. Steve! Thanks for calling.

STEVE: Yeah.

JAKE BARLOW: Who's next?

Conversation
between Dr. Albert Seymour and
Dr. Gertrude Doane

DR. SEYMOUR: Gert, Albert Seymour here. Look, I got a call from Gloria Harland about this boy who was suspended for singing.

DR. DOANE: Al, I told you, that's *not* why the boy was suspended.

DR. SEYMOUR: Maybe yes. Maybe no. That's not what's at stake here. I've got this budget. . . . Now listen. She was at a meeting last night at which this guy, Ted Griffen—

DR. DOANE: He's running for the school board.

DR. SEYMOUR. Exactly. And wouldn't you know, he's making speeches about the incident, claiming it's school policy to keep kids from singing—

DR. DOANE: Al, that's absolutely untrue.

DR. SEYMOUR: Gert, you know as well as I, it doesn't matter if it's true or not true. It's what people are saying that's important. Will be saying. Who's involved in this thing?

DR. DOANE: Joe Palleni, Peg Narwin, myself.

DR. SEYMOUR: I want a report on my desk—a report I can read out. So make it short and to the point. Soon as you can.

DR. DOANE: Al . . .

DR. SEYMOUR: Gert, believe me. I'm sensitive to this sort of thing. Just do as I've requested.

111
■

Transcript
from the Jake Barlow Talk Show

JAKE BARLOW: Okay. Who's this?

CALLER: My name is Liz.

JAKE BARLOW: Liz baby! How you doing?

LIZ: Just fine.

JAKE BARLOW: Liz, what's on your pretty mind this morning?

LIZ: Jake, I'm a mother. I have three kids. All school-age. But if I had a teacher like that—

JAKE BARLOW: Whoa! Back off. Like who?

LIZ: The one who forbade that child to show his patriotism in school. . . .

JAKE BARLOW: Right.

LIZ: I'd take my kids out of school.

JAKE BARLOW: You would?

LIZ: No question about it.

JAKE BARLOW: What about the teacher?

LIZ: Wouldn't let my kids go back to that school unless she was removed.

JAKE BARLOW: The teacher doesn't have rights?

112   LIZ: It's a free country. But what I'm saying is that she has no right to do what she does. My husband was in the military. She's taking away rights. Like the flag thing.

JAKE BARLOW: Then you know.

LIZ: I do.

Conversation between Robert Duval,
Reporter for the *St. Louis Post-Dispatch*,
and Dr. Gertrude Doane

MR. DUVAL: Is this Miss Doane, principal of Harrison High School?

DR. DOANE: Yes. Dr. Doane.

MR. DUVAL: Thank you. Of course. Dr. Doane, my name is Robert Duval. I'm a reporter with the *St. Louis Post-Dispatch*.

DR. DOANE: St. Louis?

MR. DUVAL: That's right. I'm calling from St. Louis, Missouri. I'm attempting to follow up on an AAP release that indicates your school suspended a student because he sang "The Star-Spangled Banner."

DR. DOANE: Did you say St. Louis?

MR. DUVAL: Yes, ma'am. Took the story off the wire service. And we ran it. Now you see, we have a convention going on here, our state American Legion convention. Someone there noticed this item and called the paper to see if we had any more information about the situation.

DR. DOANE: Are you serious?

MR. DUVAL: Certainly am. Would you care to hear the story we ran?

DR. DOANE: Ah . . . yes.

MR. DUVAL: The headline reads "KICKED OUT OF SCHOOL FOR PATRIOTISM." 113

DR. DOANE: Good grief!

MR. DUVAL: Yes, ma'am. Let me read you the rest. "Harrison, New Hampshire. A tenth grader was suspended from his local school because he sang 'The Star-Spangled Banner' during the school's morning exercises. The boy, Philip Malloy, who wished to sing in the spirit of patriotism, was then forced to remain home alone, since both his parents work. English teacher Margaret Narwin, who brought about the suspension, maintains the boy was making a nuisance of himself." That's it.

DR. DOANE: My God. . . . Is that being sent out over the whole country?

MR. DUVAL: Well, actually, *has* been sent out. And I thought to call and get your response. Would you like to comment, ma'am?

DR. DOANE: Full of mistakes. For a start he's a *ninth* grader. . . . Look, can I get back to you?

MR. DUVAL: Aren't you in a position to respond now?

DR. DOANE: There has been some great mistake, and . . . None of this is true.

MR. DUVAL: None of it? The boy was not suspended, then?

DR. DOANE: Yes, suspended, but not for those reasons. Look, Mr. Duval, I have to sort this out.

MR. DUVAL: When can I call back?

DR. DOANE: Give me a few hours.

MR. DUVAL: Yes, ma'am.

9:32 A.M.

Transcript
from the Jake Barlow Talk Show

JAKE BARLOW: Back again. Who's on?

CALLER: This is Roger.

JAKE BARLOW: Roger Rabbit?

ROGER: Not quite.

JAKE BARLOW: How many kids do you have?

ROGER: Ahhh . . . two.

JAKE BARLOW: Get hopping, Roger, get hopping. Ha! Okay, Roger, what's on your mind?

ROGER: About all these calls you're getting, the boy who was kicked out.

JAKE BARLOW: Makes me sick. *Sick!*

ROGER: Well, you've read the news story a few times, so I think I've understood it. And it just seems to me that that couldn't be the whole story.

JAKE BARLOW: What do you mean?

ROGER: Well, the story is slanted from the point of view of the boy. It doesn't really indicate what the teacher's position is.

JAKE BARLOW: Roger—let me get this right you are defending this so-called teacher?

ROGER: No, I didn't say that. I'm not defending anyone. The story you read is just the boy's, not the teacher's. Why should we assume that the teacher is wrong?

JAKE BARLOW: Come on. Give us a break. The kid was suspended, right?

ROGER: So it would appear.

JAKE BARLOW: Suspended for singing the national anthem, right?

ROGER: That's the story you read.

JAKE BARLOW: Now, how could singing the national anthem—*Oh, say, can you see* . . .—ever . . . ever . . . *ever* be making a nuisance?

ROGER: Well . . .

115

JAKE BARLOW: Roger, what's your point? Let me make a guess. You're a teacher!

ROGER: Actually, I'm a salesman.

JAKE BARLOW: What do you sell?

ROGER: That doesn't make—

JAKE BARLOW: Come on! Out with it! Admit it.

ROGER: Well, books, but . . .

JAKE BARLOW: Yeah, see, exactly. And here you are defending this creep of a teacher. What does the kid know other than his own, natural-born patriotism? And then this *creep* of a teacher comes along and squelches it. And this country has all these problems with morality, drugs, pornography. No way, José. Hey, Roger, you saying pornography is only a nuisance?

ROGER: But—

JAKE BARLOW: Good-bye! Always the one rotten apple. Hey, out there. Do you agree with this guy? Tell you what! Why don't you out there—let's start a crusade—I want you all—if you feel anything about all this—to *write* to the teacher. Hey, free country! Do you agree with what she did? Okay, tell her. If you disagree, tell her that. Let's see, here's her name, Margaret Narwin. Margaret Narwin. N–a–r–w–i–n. Harrison, New Hampshire. Let her know what you think. You agree with that guy? Just write her. Postcard. *Brick*. Hey, just kidding. Something. Okay! Now this. . . .

116

Conversation
among Dr. Gertrude Doane,
Margaret Narwin,
and Dr. Joseph Palleni

DR. DOANE: Peg, just tell me what happened.

MISS NARWIN: I've told you twice now.

DR. DOANE: I know you're upset, Peg. But I have to get it down clearly. Anyway, we all need to tell the same story.

DR. PALLENI: Amen. Gert's trying to be helpful, Peg.

MISS NARWIN: It's terribly upsetting.

DR. DOANE: Well, yes. . . . To all of us. Now, once more. Please.

MISS NARWIN: Very well. . . . Philip Malloy—from the first day he entered my homeroom—last week—during the time the students are asked to stand in silence—

DR. PALLENI: The rule is, "Respectful silence." I looked it up. It's in your memo about opening exercises. Isn't in the student handbook. But I think it should be.

DR. DOANE: Good point.

MISS NARWIN: During the playing of the national anthem, he sang. Loudly. With no respect. Very loudly. To make a commotion. Obviously. The first time he did it, I asked him to stop, and he did. After a bit. The second two times, he didn't. Refused. That's when I sent him to Joe. Both times.

DR. PALLENI: The boy admitted it, Gert. No bones about that.

MISS NARWIN: Deliberately provocative.

DR. DOANE: Do we know why? Peg?

117

MISS NARWIN: I haven't the slightest idea.

DR. DOANE: Joe?

DR. PALLENI: Nope. No problems before. Ever.

DR. DOANE: Maybe I should talk to some students.

DR. PALLENI: Witnesses.

MISS NARWIN: I don't know. I will say this, Gert, he's always been restless in English class. Sort of a wise guy, I'd have to call him. Trying to cover up laziness with smart talk. I don't know why. Sometimes that just happens. The chemistry. In his last exam for me he wrote a very foolish, really provocative, answer. Mocking me.

DR. DOANE: You?

MISS NARWIN: Oh, yes. Absolutely. Mocking.

DR. DOANE: Do you still have it?

MISS NARWIN: I always return exams to students.

DR. DOANE: Too bad. But there must be some reason—

MISS NARWIN: I agree.

DR. PALLENI: Home, Gert. Home. Ninety-nine point nine times out of a hundred, you get a thing like this, a kid acting out, believe me, it's home. Acting out here for what's happening there.

DR. DOANE: But we don't know that.

DR. PALLENI: Hey, what's the difference? They always blame the school. You know that.

DR. DOANE: Well, as far as I'm concerned, this is strictly a discipline problem. That's what I intend to tell people. Do we agree?

118

DR. PALLENI: Well, the thing is, it's the truth.

MISS NARWIN: I didn't think it was wise to suspend him.

DR. PALLENI: Two infractions in one week, Peg. Right?

That's the rule. You sent him out. To me. If we start bending the rules each time . . .

MISS NARWIN: What could I have done?

DR. PALLENI: Only trying to be supportive.

MISS NARWIN: I know.

DR. DOANE: It'll blow over.

DR. PALLENI: Sure thing.

DR. DOANE: Joe, write up a draft of something—keep strictly to the facts—to give to Seymour. Do it immediately. I want to speak to some students.

11:00 A.M.

Written by Dr. Joseph Palleni

MEMO

HARRISON SCHOOL DISTRICT

Where Our Children Are Educated, Not Just Taught

Dr. Albert Seymour
Superintendent

Mrs. Gloria Harland
Chairman, School Board

TO: SEYMOUR
FROM: DOANE
RE: SUSPENSION OF PHILIP MALLOY

1. Each morning—during homeroom period—the national anthem is played over the high school announcement system.

2. At such times students are asked: "Please all rise and stand at *respectful, silent* attention . . ."

3. On March 28, March 29, and March 30, Philip Malloy caused a disturbance in his homeroom class (Margaret Narwin, teacher) by singing the national anthem in a loud, raucous, *disrespectful* manner.

4. When asked by Miss Narwin—on the first occasion—to cease, Philip Malloy reluctantly did so. But on the second and third occasions, he refused and was sent to Assistant Principal Joe Palleni for discipline.

5. Philip Malloy does not dispute the above facts.

6. On the third occurrence, Philip Malloy was asked to promise not to show such a disrespectful attitude, and to apologize to the teacher and to his fellow classmates. *He refused.*

7. Dr. Palleni, following his principal's guidelines, therefore suspended Philip Malloy from class for two days in hopes that he would learn to show proper respect toward the national anthem, school, teacher, and fellow students.

8. It should be noted that Philip Malloy was reported to show inappropriate behavior in his regular English classes with Miss Narwin.

11:15 A.M.

Conversation
between Dr. Gertrude Doane
and Ken Barchet

DR. DOANE: Ken, I'm trying to understand what happened there. That morning. Is this clear?

KEN BARCHET: Yes.

DR. DOANE: And you were with him. I hope you can speak freely. I'm just trying to work it out.

KEN BARCHET: Sure.

DR. DOANE: So, in your view—what occurred?

KEN BARCHET: Well, you know, the tape, the music went on—

DR. DOANE: Which day was this?

KEN BARCHET: Wednesday.

DR. DOANE: Okay. Wednesday. Go on.

KEN BARCHET: Right. The music went on. And we were just standing there. We're supposed to. And the next thing, Miss Narwin was telling Philip to stop.

DR. DOANE: Stop what?

KEN BARCHET: I'm not sure. The newspaper said singing.

DR. DOANE: What about the other days?

KEN BARCHET: You know, he was, again, sort of, I guess, singing.

DR. DOANE: In what way?

KEN BARCHET: Just singing.

DR. DOANE: Loudly?

KEN BARCHET: Well, not really.

DR. DOANE: But you heard him?

KEN BARCHET: I guess.

DR. DOANE: How close to Philip do you sit?

KEN BARCHET: 'Cross the room.

DR. DOANE: So, loudly enough for you to hear?

KEN BARCHET: Well . . .

DR. DOANE: Then what happened?

KEN BARCHET: Miss Narwin got mad.

DR. DOANE: Why?

KEN BARCHET: Well, you know, like you said, Philip was singing. And I guess we're not supposed to.

DR. DOANE: Did Philip stop?

KEN BARCHET: Yeah. When she told him to get out.

DR. DOANE: Not before?

KEN BARCHET: No.

DR. DOANE: What did the class do?

KEN BARCHET: I wasn't paying attention.

11:45 A.M.

Phone Conversation from
Harrison High School Pay Phone
between Ken Barchet and Philip Malloy

KEN BARCHET: Hey, man, what's happening?

PHILIP MALLOY: Nothing. It's boring. What's happening there?

KEN BARCHET: Just spoke to Doane.

PHILIP MALLOY: The principal?

KEN BARCHET: Yeah.

PHILIP MALLOY: How come?

KEN BARCHET: She called me in to find out what happened.

PHILIP MALLOY: What you tell her?

KEN BARCHET: What happened. The whole thing. Lot of people talking about it. You know, with the newspaper and all.

PHILIP MALLOY: Yeah, but what did you tell her?

122
■

KEN BARCHET: I thought I should tell her how funny it was.

PHILIP MALLOY: Come on! What did you tell her?

KEN BARCHET: Nothing. I mean, it wasn't anything. I don't know why they're making a fuss about it.

PHILIP MALLOY: I still have English with her, but they switched me back to Lunser's homeroom.

KEN BARCHET: He's okay. Tells good jokes. Someone told me he has a collection of joke books. That's where he gets all those one-liners.

PHILIP MALLOY: That true?

KEN BARCHET: Nick told me. We going to work out this afternoon?

PHILIP MALLOY: Yeah.

KEN BARCHET: Catch you later.

11:50 A.M.

Conversation
between Dr. Gertrude Doane
and Cynthia Gambia, Student

DR. DOANE: Cynthia, what I'm trying to do is understand what happened in Miss Narwin's homeroom class. With Philip Malloy. When these incidents occurred. I hope you can tell me exactly what you saw. I'm trying to work it out.

CYNTHIA GAMBIA: Yes. I understand. I wasn't paying much attention.

123

DR. DOANE: That's all right. Go on. Tell me what happened as you saw it.

CYNTHIA GAMBIA: Well, during "The Star-Spangled Banner"—when the tape went on—Philip started to hum.

DR. DOANE: *Hum?*

CYNTHIA GAMBIA: I think so.

DR. DOANE: Not sing?

CYNTHIA GAMBIA: I'm not sure. It could have been. I wasn't paying attention. Not at first. Not the first time.

DR. DOANE: And then?

CYNTHIA GAMBIA: Miss Narwin asked him to leave.

DR. DOANE: Which days were these?

CYNTHIA GAMBIA: All three.

DR. DOANE: Was Philip causing a disturbance?

CYNTHIA GAMBIA: Well, I heard him. Sort of. I mean, it wasn't loud or anything. Not like the paper said. But he wouldn't stop. And she did ask him. I guess that was the disturbance.

DR. DOANE: So he wasn't loud.

CYNTHIA GAMBIA: Maybe the last time.

DR. DOANE: Very loud?

CYNTHIA GAMBIA: Well, loud.

DR. DOANE: What day was that?

CYNTHIA GAMBIA: Ah . . . Tuesday. Or Thursday. I'm not sure.

DR. DOANE: What did the other students do?

CYNTHIA GAMBIA: Nothing. I don't think they knew anything was going to happen. If they did, they would have watched.

124

DR. DOANE: Do you have any idea why he—Philip—did this?

CYNTHIA GAMBIA: No.

DR. DOANE: Did you want to add anything else?

CYNTHIA GAMBIA: No. I guess not. I mean, he *was* being sort of rude.

DR. DOANE: Philip?

CYNTHIA GAMBIA: Miss Narwin did ask him to stop. You're supposed to be quiet. Everybody says that's the rule. He certainly wasn't. She's a fair teacher. All the kids say so.

12:30 P.M.

From a Speech Delivered by Ted Griffen
to a Lunch Meeting
of the Harrison Rotary Club

MR. GRIFFEN: . . . so what I will try to do—if elected as a member of the Harrison School Board—is not just keep the cost of education down to a reasonable level—I'm talking here of keeping our taxes down—I will work with the rest of the board to support basic American values. But let me tell you good people—and I am sure I speak for you too—I am shocked that a Harrison student should be expelled from one of our schools simply because he desires to sing the national anthem. Yes, my friends, it is true. It has happened here. Here—in yesterday's *Record* is the full story. Shocking. What I say is—most emphatically—what is the point of installing computers—which my generation never seemed to need—and at great cost—if our young people are not allowed to practice the elemental values of American patriotism? Is that the way we budget our education dollars?

Conversation
between Dr. Gertrude Doane
and Allison Doresett

DR. DOANE: Allison, I'm working hard to understand what happened in Miss Narwin's class. The incident with Philip Malloy.

ALLISON DORESETT: I know. Lot of kids are talking about it.

DR. DOANE: What are they saying?

ALLISON DORESETT: About how big a thing it is.

DR. DOANE: Do you think it is?

ALLISON DORESETT: I don't know. Maybe. If they pay all that attention. I mean, someone said the TV would be here.

DR. DOANE: I hope not. Now, as I understand it, you are in Miss Narwin's homeroom class.

ALLISON DORESETT: I have English with her too.

DR. DOANE: I'm talking about homeroom.

ALLISON DORESETT: I have her.

DR. DOANE: So you were there all three times?

ALLISON DORESETT: Uh-huh.

DR. DOANE: Tell me what you saw.

ALLISON DORESETT: Well, Philip, he doesn't like Miss Narwin.

DR. DOANE: He doesn't?

ALLISON DORESETT: I don't think so.

DR. DOANE: Just think? Do you know why?

126

ALLISON DORESETT: It's what people are saying. In class—English class—he just sits there, you know, like he's bored and can't stand anything she says. It's just the way he looks. On his face. You know. But then he suddenly makes some remark, a joke or something. Something funny.

DR. DOANE: Do you think this has anything to do with what happened?

ALLISON DORESETT: Well, it was so obvious he was trying to get at her.

DR. DOANE: What do you mean?

ALLISON DORESETT: Get her mad.

DR. DOANE: Because he doesn't like her?

ALLISON DORESETT: He's been so moody lately. Those times in homeroom—I think he was doing it to get Miss Narwin in trouble.

DR. DOANE: I wish you'd tell me more about that.

ALLISON DORESETT: Well, he's been angry a lot lately. I go home on the same bus with him. The other day I—you know—tried to sit next to him. On the bus. He was looking all angry. I tried to talk to him.

DR. DOANE: And?

ALLISON DORESETT: He got all angry. Wouldn't talk to me.

DR. DOANE: Do you know why?

ALLISON DORESETT: That's the way he is.

DR. DOANE: Allison, I appreciate your help.

ALLISON DORESETT: Can I say something?

DR. DOANE: Of course.

ALLISON DORESETT: I like Miss Narwin.

DR. DOANE: I'm glad. Your telling the truth can only help her.

MEMO

HARRISON SCHOOL DISTRICT

Where Our Children Are Educated, Not Just Taught

Dr. Albert Seymour
Superintendent

Mrs. Gloria Harland
Chairman, School Board

TO: DR. A. SEYMOUR
FROM: DR. G. DOANE
RE: SUSPENSION OF PHILIP MALLOY

1. Each and every morning—during homeroom period—the national anthem is played over the high school announcement system.

2. At such times all students are asked, to quote the standard district guide, "Please all rise and stand at *respectful*, silent attention. . . ." At no time in the history of this procedure has any disturbance been recorded.

3. On March 28, March 29, and March 30, Philip Malloy deliberately caused a disturbance in his homeroom class (Margaret Narwin, teacher) by singing the national anthem in a loud, raucous, *disrespectful* fashion, thereby drawing attention to himself.

4. When requested by Miss Narwin—on the first occasion—to cease, Philip Malloy did so, albeit reluctantly. On the second and third occasions, he repeated his disrespectful behavior, and when he refused to stop, he was sent—standard procedure—to Assistant Principal Dr. Joseph Palleni for discipline.

128
■

5. Philip Malloy did not dispute the above facts.

6. A random selection of students—who were in the classroom at the time—confirms these events. Indeed, there is evidence that Philip Malloy's acts were indicative of some personal animosity he feels toward the homeroom teacher, Miss Narwin. His rudeness was also on display in the English classes he had with her. His grade there indicates inferior work.

7. On the third occurrence, Philip Malloy was asked 1) to promise not to show such a disrespectful attitude toward our national anthem and 2) to apologize to his teacher and his classmates for his behavior. He refused, choosing the option afforded him of suspension.

8. Dr. Palleni, following district guidelines approved by the Superintendent, therefore suspended Philip Malloy from class for two days in hopes that he would learn to show proper respect toward the national anthem, his school, his teacher, and his fellow students.

DR. GERTRUDE DOANE
Principal

2:22 P.M.

Telegram to Margaret Narwin
Held by Harrison High School Office

TO: MARGARET NARWIN, HARRISON,
    NEW HAMPSHIRE, HIGH SCHOOL
FROM: YOUNG AMERICANS FOR
    AMERICA

On behalf of our membership we strongly con-
demn your suppression of patriotism in the
American School System.

Sincerely,
Jessica Wittington, Executive Secretary
Tampa, Florida

3:05 P.M.

Telegram Delivered to Philip Malloy

TO: PHILIP MALLOY
FROM: SOCIETY FOR THE
    PRESERVATION OF FREE SPEECH

We applaud your defense of the freedom of
speech in a public arena. One is never too
young to fight for our constitutional rights,
which are under constant assault from right-
wing forces. Stand firm. Stand tall. Please call
upon us for active support.

Hank Morgan
Chicago, Illinois

3:15 P.M.

Telegram Delivered to Dr. Gertrude Doane

TO: PRINCIPAL, HARRISON HIGH

People like Margaret Marwin should be kicked
out of teaching.

Charles Elderson
Woodbank, North Carolina

3:30 P.M.

Written by Dr. Albert Seymour

MEMO

HARRISON SCHOOL DISTRICT

Where Our Children Are Educated, Not Just Taught

Dr. Albert Seymour
Superintendent

Mrs. Gloria Harland
Chairman, School Board

TO: MRS. GLORIA HARLAND,
    CHAIRMAN, SCHOOL BOARD
FROM: DR. A. SEYMOUR
RE: SUSPENSION OF PHILIP MALLOY

1. It is the practice in *all* Harrison schools that each and
every morning—during homeroom period—the national
anthem is played over the announcement systems. It is

part of our general ongoing program of support for traditional American values.

2. At such times all students are asked to "Please all rise and stand at *respectful*, silent attention. . . ." In past years our desire for a dignified moment of patriotism has been firmly maintained. At no time in the history of this program has any disturbance been recorded.

3. On March 28, March 29, and March 30, Philip Malloy deliberately caused a disturbance in his homeroom class (Margaret Narwin, a teacher of twenty years' standing) by singing the national anthem in a loud, raucous, *disrespectful* fashion, thereby drawing attention to himself and away from the words. There are strong indications that he was acting out some personal animosity toward the teacher in question for reasons unknown. His school performance has been inferior. (It has been suggested that there may be problems in the home arena. Please note, however, that the law *requires* schools to keep such personal information confidential.)

4. When requested by his teacher, Miss Narwin, on the first occasion to maintain a dignified response to the national anthem, Philip Malloy did so, though reluctantly. On the second and third occasions, he repeated his disrespectful acts, and when he refused to stop, he was—as a matter of course—sent to Assistant Principal Dr. Joseph Palleni for discipline.

5. Philip Malloy—when given the opportunity—did *not* dispute the above facts.

6. Students who were in the classroom at the time of the incidents confirm these events.

7. On the third occurrence, Philip Malloy was requested 1) to promise that he would show an attitude of respect toward our national anthem and 2) to apologize to his

teacher and his classmates for his rude behavior. He refused, choosing the option of suspension *himself*.

8. Dr. Palleni, following district guidelines approved by the School Board, therefore suspended Philip Malloy from class for two days in hopes that he would learn to show proper respect toward the national anthem and his school, teacher, and fellow students.

DR. A. SEYMOUR
Superintendent of Schools

6:20 P.M.

Conversation
between Philip Malloy's Parents

MR. MALLOY: Hi! Where's Philip?

MRS. MALLOY: He just got in. Washing up.

MR. MALLOY: People were talking about him today. Amazing how many folks saw that thing in the paper.

MRS. MALLOY: At my place too.

MR. MALLOY: Makes you feel good.

MRS. MALLOY: We should celebrate.

Discussion
between Philip Malloy and His Parents
During Dinner

MR. MALLOY: Well, how do you feel?

PHILIP MALLOY: Okay.

MRS. MALLOY: You should be pleased with yourself.

MR. MALLOY: What do you think of that telegram?

PHILIP MALLOY: I don't know. Who are they? I never heard of them before.

MR. MALLOY: They've heard of you. You're famous.

PHILIP MALLOY: How?

MRS. MALLOY: In the news, wasn't it?

PHILIP MALLOY: You think so?

MR. MALLOY: Sure. Just shows you. One person makes a difference. One person standing up for what he believes in.

MRS. MALLOY: I'm just so glad it's worked out all right. Aren't you?

PHILIP MALLOY: I suppose.

MR. MALLOY: What's the problem now?

PHILIP MALLOY: Be weird going back. What kids will say.

MR. MALLOY: They'll be on your side. You said they all hated that woman. Just make sure you sing in the morning. People will look to that.

PHILIP MALLOY: I'll be in Mr. Lunser's class.

MR. MALLOY: You said he likes kids singing.

PHILIP MALLOY: Sort of.

MR. MALLOY: I think you should go over and speak to Ted Griffen too.

PHILIP MALLOY: Why?

MR. MALLOY: Someone at work heard him at some speech he gave—the school board thing—he mentioned this whole business. . . .

PHILIP MALLOY: He did?

MRS. MALLOY: And he brought in that reporter.

MR. MALLOY: Come on, Philip, people are really on your side!

PHILIP MALLOY: I guess.

7:30 P.M.

From a Speech Delivered by Ted Griffen to a Meeting of the Harrison Chamber of Commerce

---

MR. GRIFFEN: Before I get into my formal speech, I'd like to lead off—put it right at the top of your thoughts—with something that has happened here in Harrison, something that has disturbed me greatly. I am a great believer in basic American values. And let me tell you good people—and I am sure I speak for you too—I am shocked that a Harrison student should be expelled from one of our schools because he desires to sing the national anthem. Yes, my friends, it is the truth. It has happened here. Here—in yesterday's *Record* is the full story. Shocking. What I say is—most emphatically—what is the point of installing computers—which my generation never seemed to need—and at great cost—if our young

135

people are not allowed to practice the elemental values of American patriotism? And to think—because this story—so I understand—this has been picked up by the national press—how shocking it is that this is the way our town of Harrison should come to be known. It should not be condoned!

8:02 P.M.

Phone Conversation between Margaret Narwin and Her Sister, Anita Wigham

---

MISS NARWIN: Hello?

ANITA WIGHAM: Peg!

MISS NARWIN: Anita, yes, dear, what is it? What's the matter?

ANITA WIGHAM: I . . . I . . .

MISS NARWIN: What is it?

ANITA WIGHAM: I was just reading the evening paper—and right on page one . . . is this story—it's this story about you!

MISS NARWIN: What are you talking about?

ANITA WIGHAM: It's right *here*.

MISS NARWIN: Are you sure?

ANITA WIGHAM: Absolutely sure. It must be everywhere.

MISS NARWIN: What does it say?

ANITA WIGHAM: I'll read it. It's so awful, Peg. It says, "KICKED OUT OF SCHOOL FOR PATRIOTISM." That's the headline. It's just one of those boxed stories. But it's on the front page. "Harrison, New Hampshire. AAP. A tenth grader was suspended from his local school because he sang 'The Star-Spangled Banner' during the school's morning exercises. The boy, Philip Malloy, who wished to sing in the spirit of patriotism, was then forced to remain home alone, since both his parents work. English teacher Margaret Narwin, who brought about the suspension, maintains the boy was making a nuisance of himself." Peg, I don't understand. Peg?

MISS NARWIN: I . . .

ANITA WIGHAM: But why—

MISS NARWIN: And this was in *your* newspaper?

ANITA WIGHAM: Peg, I'm *holding* it.

MISS NARWIN: Dear God. . . .

ANITA WIGHAM: It's not true, is it?

MISS NARWIN: No. None of it.

ANITA WIGHAM: But where does it come from?

MISS NARWIN: Let me call you back. In a few moments.

8:10 P.M.

Phone Conversation between Margaret Narwin and Dr. Gertrude Doane

---

DR. DOANE: Yes, Peg, hello. How are you?

MISS NARWIN: Gert, I . . .

DR. DOANE: Peg, are you all right?

MISS NARWIN: Gert, I just got a call from my sister—in Florida—about a newspaper story—published there—about this business—

DR. DOANE: I know, Peg. I've already heard about it.

MISS NARWIN: But I—

DR. DOANE: I just didn't see any point in upsetting you any more.

MISS NARWIN: But why?

DR. DOANE: I already received a call from some midwestern reporter. There have been telegrams—

MISS NARWIN: Telegrams?

DR. DOANE: At school. I told the office to hold them. Peg, it's gotten out of hand. I don't know how. It seems there are these radio talk shows—

MISS NARWIN: I want to see them. What do the telegrams say?

DR. DOANE: Well, they believe what the story says and . . . Believe me, Peg, I know. It's all a mistake.

MISS NARWIN: Were they addressed to me? Personally?

DR. DOANE: Well, to me, and yes, some to you, but—

MISS NARWIN: I want to see them.

DR. DOANE: I don't think—

MISS NARWIN: I don't understand any of this.

DR. DOANE: Peg, I assure you, I have complete confidence in you.

MISS NARWIN: It's so monstrous, so . . .

DR. DOANE: Yes, I agree.

MISS NARWIN: My sister, in Florida . . .

DR. DOANE: Peg, we're just going to have to weather it out and—maybe you'll want to take the day off tomorrow.

MISS NARWIN: No. I can't give in to this—

DR. DOANE: Peg, believe me. It will calm down.

From the Diary of Philip Malloy

Weird day not doing much. Got these telegrams from these people I never heard of before, talking about something I don't get. Folks all high. Be glad to be back in school. I hate sitting around. Glad to be in Lunser's homeroom class again. Get things back to normal. Guess I'll still be in Narwin's English. Better speak to her and see if I can do some extra work. So I can get on the track team. Wonder what she'll say?

Did some extra time on Dad's rowing machine.

I'm a little nervous.

16

Tuesday, April 3

Letter Sent to Margaret Narwin

To Margaret Narwin,

These days there is so much talk about young people and education. It seems to me that people like you—who don't believe in patriotism—cause the problems. You should find a better profession for your lack of ability.

LINDA DORCHESTER
Ann Arbor, Michigan

Letter Sent to Margaret Narwin

Dear Margaret Narwin,

As a teacher in the Dayton, Ohio, school system for ten years, I am dismayed and horrified that in this day and age a colleague of mine should suspend a student from school for singing the national anthem. We suffer enough from unfair criticism. The profession does not need people like you who make it so hard for the rest of us.

CARLTON HAVEN
Dayton, Ohio

Letter Sent to Margaret Narwin

Margaret Narwin,

I'm a veteran who fought for his country and gave his blood and I really hate people like you.

DAVID MAIK
Eugene, Oregon

Lottor Scnt to Margaret Narwin

Margaret Narwin,

Surely you have something better to do with your classroom authority than attacking kids who express their love of our country.

LAURA JACOBS
San Diego, California

Conversation
between Dr. Albert Seymour and
Dr. Gertrude Doane
in the Superintendent's Office

DR. DOANE: How many are there?

DR. SEYMOUR: Telegrams? Ten. Fifteen. I haven't counted
exactly. I suspect more will be coming.

DR. DOANE: This one is from Idaho. Incredible!

DR. SEYMOUR: Every one of them demanding we fire this
Narwin woman.

DR. DOANE: Not this one.

DR. SEYMOUR: Well, the overwhelming majority. And I had
twelve calls at my home last night.

DR. DOANE: From whom?

DR. SEYMOUR: People in town, Gert. People who vote.
They're outraged.

DR. DOANE: And they believe that story. . . .

DR. SEYMOUR: I'm beginning to believe it.

DR. DOANE: Al!

DR. SEYMOUR: What do you expect me to do?

DR. DOANE: Support Peg Narwin.

DR. SEYMOUR: A TV network wants to interview people.

DR. DOANE: You're not going to let them. . . .

DR. SEYMOUR: No. No. Protect the privacy of minors and
all that stuff. From what I gather, talk-show hosts—
radio—have picked the story up. . . . The board wants

142
■

me to issue a statement. Gert, I have an appointment with this Ted Griffen at nine-fifteen.

DR. DOANE: Griffen is running for board. . . .

DR. SEYMOUR: Exactly. He's already made speeches about this business. Look, Gert, I'm sorry, but between you and me—quote me and I'll deny it—I don't care about the board. I can handle them. But the budget I don't need to tell you. If we lose again . . .

DR. DOANE: I know.

DR. SEYMOUR: People scream if the kids are not educated. Then they scream if you ask for the money to do it.

DR. DOANE: I know.

DR. SEYMOUR: I want to see the file on this Narwin woman.

DR. DOANE: Why?

DR. SEYMOUR: I have to decide what to do.

DR. DOANE: Before your meeting with this Griffen?

DR. SEYMOUR: Exactly. When you get to your office, send one of the secretaries over here with it.

DR. DOANE: Al . . .

DR. SEYMOUR: Gert, my job is to make sure these kids get educated. Whatever it takes. Send it.

7:30 A.M.

Conversation
between Philip Malloy and His Parents
During Breakfast

143

MR. MALLOY: You don't have to be nervous about anything. You were right. The fact that they moved you out of that woman's class proves you were right.

PHILIP MALLOY: Just homeroom. I have English with her.

MRS. MALLOY: I'm sure she won't give you any more trouble.

PHILIP MALLOY: It's just the other kids. . . .

MR. MALLOY: You said they hated her too.

PHILIP MALLOY: Yeah. . . .

MRS. MALLOY: Do you want me to drive you?

PHILIP MALLOY: No. I'm meeting Ken.

MRS. MALLOY: You'll be fine.

MR. MALLOY: You know how to make it work?

PHILIP MALLOY: No.

MR. MALLOY: Same as I've told you. Half your runs are won at the start. Head up. Leap out of the blocks. Show them what you can do.

PHILIP MALLOY: Easy for you—

MR. MALLOY: The only reason I didn't make it to the Olympics . . .

PHILIP MALLOY: I know.

MR. MALLOY: Biggest regret I've ever had was dropping out of college.

PHILIP MALLOY: You had to.

MR. MALLOY: I suppose.

MRS. MALLOY: Phil, you better go if you don't want to miss your bus.

Conversation
between Philip Malloy and Ken Barchet
on the Way to the School Bus

PHILIP MALLOY: What's happening?

KEN BARCHET: Nothing. What's with you?

PHILIP MALLOY: Not much. We going to run this afternoon?

KEN BARCHET: Can't.

PHILIP MALLOY: How come?

KEN BARCHET: Got track team right after school. Coach told us it's going to be at least three hours. You really should have tried out, man. You know that Polanski kid?

PHILIP MALLOY: Brian Polanski?

KEN BARCHET: Right. Coach has him down for the 400.

PHILIP MALLOY: Can't do anything.

KEN BARCHET: Best we got. You could.

PHILIP MALLOY: Sure.

KEN BARCHET: You mad at the coach or something?

PHILIP MALLOY: No. Why?

KEN BARCHET: You should change your mind.

PHILIP MALLOY: About what?

KEN BARCHET: Being on the team.

PHILIP MALLOY: Yeah, I might. I got Mr. Lunser for homeroom.

145

KEN BARCHET: You told me.

PHILIP MALLOY: Want to know why I didn't go out for the team?

KEN BARCHET: Okay.

PHILIP MALLOY: Narwin.

KEN BARCHET: What she have to do with it?

PHILIP MALLOY: She almost flunked me in English. That meant I wasn't allowed to try out.

KEN BARCHET: That why you're mad at her?

PHILIP MALLOY: But I'm going to ask her if I can do extra work. For credit.

KEN BARCHET: Think she'll give it to you?

PHILIP MALLOY: I don't know. No reason she shouldn't. I'll ask.

KEN BARCHET: She might be mad at you.

PHILIP MALLOY: If you just tell them you're sorry, that's all. . . .

KEN BARCHET: Be great if you could get on the team.

PHILIP MALLOY: That's what I've been saying.

7:45 A.M.

Conversation
between Margaret Narwin and
Dr. Gertrude Doane

MISS NARWIN: I don't believe it.

DR. DOANE: It is incredible.

146

MISS NARWIN: How many telegrams are there?

DR. DOANE: Here?

MISS NARWIN: Yes.

DR. DOANE: Almost two hundred.

MISS NARWIN: There will be letters. . . .

DR. DOANE: Well . . . The superintendent's office put out a statement explaining the true situation.

MISS NARWIN: What did he say?

DR. DOANE: Peg, you have to accept the idea that it's all a misunderstanding.

MISS NARWIN: Easy for you to say.

DR. DOANE: You can't blame yourself. . . .

MISS NARWIN: I pleaded with Joe not to suspend him.

DR. DOANE: I know you said that. We've issued a statement. I think it's good.

MISS NARWIN: May I see it?

DR. DOANE: Of course. Here. What's the matter?

MISS NARWIN: This statement doesn't support me.

DR. DOANE: Peg, it does.

MISS NARWIN: Where?

DR. DOANE: Peg, understand that—

MISS NARWIN: Will the boy be in school today?

DR. DOANE: I suppose. . . . I need to tell you I said no to some TV people.

MISS NARWIN: No. Absolutely not.

DR. DOANE: Exactly. They can't come in without permission. Peg, do you want to take the day off?

MISS NARWIN: No. They'll come to my home.

DR. DOANE: It's perfectly understandable.

147

MISS NARWIN: Gert, I don't understand. I don't. I have been teaching—

DR. DOANE: People believe what they read.

MISS NARWIN: I have my class. . . .

DR. DOANE: Peg, as of this morning I've moved Philip from your English class. He's with Mr. Keegan.

MISS NARWIN: Why did you do that?

DR. DOANE: Probably for the best. . . .

MISS NARWIN: Best for whom?

DR. DOANE: For you. The boy—

MISS NARWIN: Gert, people will misconstrue.

DR. DOANE: We are trying to be evenhanded. . . .

MISS NARWIN: He's a student. I'm a teacher. Hands are not meant to be even.

DR. DOANE: That's my decision.

7:55 A.M.

Conversation
between Philip Malloy and Allison Doresett

ALLISON DORESETT: Philip!

PHILIP MALLOY: Oh, hi.

ALLISON DORESETT: I just want you to know that I think what you did was really mean.

PHILIP MALLOY: What?

ALLISON DORESETT: Narwin is one of the best teachers. All the kids say so. It's really embarrassing.

148

PHILIP MALLOY: What are you talking about?

ALLISON DORESETT: You were just doing that to annoy her.

PHILIP MALLOY: Who?

ALLISON DORESETT: Miss Narwin. Everybody knows it. She's so fair.

PHILIP MALLOY: That's not true! Well, if you're not even going to listen . . . !

8:00 A.M.

MEMO

HARRISON SCHOOL DISTRICT

Where Our Children Are Educated, Not Just Taught

Dr. Albert Seymour
Superintendent

Mrs. Gloria Harland
Chairman, School Board

OFFICIAL STATEMENT

It is the practice in *all* Harrison schools that during morning exercises the national anthem is played, part of our program in support of traditional American values.

There is *no* rule that prohibits a student from singing along if he/she so desires.

The Harrison School District is pleased to *encourage* appropriate displays of patriotism.

It is the responsibility of our classroom teachers to monitor student behavior in this regard.

8:03 A.M.

Discussion
in Bernard Lunser's Homeroom Class

MR. LUNSER: Let's go! Let's go! Seats! My God, it's Philip

Malloy, Harrison High's own Uncle Sam. Take any empty seat, Philip. I'll set it later.

INTERCOM VOICE OF DR. GERTRUDE DOANE, HARRISON HIGH PRINCIPAL: Good morning to all students, faculty, and staff. Today is Tuesday, April 3. Today will be a Schedule B day.

MR. LUNSER: That's B for bozos, boys and girls. B!

DR. DOANE: Today in history: on this day, in the year 1366, King Henry IV of England was born.

MR. LUNSER: Not to be confused with a fifth of scotch.

DR. DOANE: Today in 1860, the pony express began.

MR. LUNSER: Faster than today's PO.

DR. DOANE: April 3, in 1961, actor Eddie Murphy was born.

MR. LUNSER: Eddie Murphy. My only competition.

DR. DOANE: Please all rise and stand at respectful, silent attention for the playing of our national anthem.

MR. LUNSER: Philip!

PHILIP MALLOY: What?

MR. LUNSER: You want to sing?

STUDENT: Yeah, sing!

MR. LUNSER: Keep the lip buttoned, Brian! Philip?

PHILIP MALLOY: No. . . .

MR. LUNSER: Okay. Just want to make sure your rights are protected.

Oh, say, can you see by the dawn's early light,
What so proudly we hailed at the twilight's last gleaming?
Whose broad stripes and bright stars, thro' the perilous fight,
O'er the ramparts we watched were so gallantly streaming? . . .

MR. LUNSER: You sure, Philip?

PHILIP MALLOY: Yeah. . . .

And the rockets' red glare, the bombs bursting in air,
Gave proof thro' the night that our flag was still there.
Oh, say does that star-spangled banner yet wave
O'er the land of the free and the home of the brave?

8:15 A.M.

Phone Conversation
between Dr. Gertrude Doane and
Robert Duval, Reporter,
the *St. Louis Post-Dispatch*

MR. DUVAL: But that's just it. I've heard your superinten
dent's statement.

DR. DOANE: Mr. Duval, I am trying to run a school here
with more than four hundred students.

MR. DUVAL: Well, ma'am, I spoke to your local reporter,
the woman who broke the story. Ms. Stewart? She gave
it to me. Would you like me to quote from the statement?

DR. DOANE: Mr. Duval, I know what it says.

MR. DUVAL: Now, it's not exactly in support of your Miss
Narwin, is it. Would you agree?

DR. DOANE: Mr. Duval, I really don't think there's anything
more to say.

MR. DUVAL: What I'm hearing, ma'am, is that you're not
altogether happy with the statement.

DR. DOANE: I did *not* say that.

MR. DUVAL: I understand. But wouldn't this teacher—this
Miss Narwin—like her side of the story set out?

DR. DOANE: I can't speak for her. She's a fine person who—

MR. DUVAL: Dr. Doane, I hope I can understand your con-

151

flict. But if I'm understanding this correctly there's something like a shift going on here. Against the teacher. Now, I don't have to go through you. I could approach her.

DR. DOANE: Why are you so interested?

MR. DUVAL: I sense there's something more here. I'm not even sure what. I confess that interests me. I sure would appreciate your cooperation.

DR. DOANE: I would have to ask her.

MR. DUVAL: I understand. But I am prepared to fly East right away.

DR. DOANE: Give me your number again.

MR. DUVAL: Sure thing.

8:16 A.M.

Conversations
between Philip Malloy and Students
in the Hallway on the Way to First Class

TODD BECKER: Hey, Philip, what's happening, man?

PHILIP MALLOY: Nothing.

TODD BECKER: You going to have a press conference?

PHILIP MALLOY: Get off!

JOSEPH CRIPPENS: Look out! Here comes Uncle Sam! That's what Mr. Lunser called him.

AMY DEVER: What's it like to be famous?

SUSAN FOWLER: Newspapers and all . . .

PHILIP MALLOY: Come on. I have to get to class.

JOSEPH CRIPPENS: Let the big man go.

JASON MARKS: Hey, Philip? How come you went after Narwin? Todd Becker said it's because you were failing English! That true?

PHILIP MALLOY: I have a class!

JOSEPH CRIPPENS: Let Uncle Sam go.

Letter Sent to Philip Malloy

Dear Philip,

We support your defense of America. Keep on singing. We all join in.

ROLANDO MERCHAUD
Red Oak, Iowa

Letter Sent to Philip Malloy

Dear Philip,

We, Miss Harbor's 4th grade class at the Robert Fulton School, like to sing "The Star-Spangled Banner" too. You can come to our school.

MS. HARBOR'S 4TH GRADE CLASS
Robert Fulton School
Brooklyn, New York

Telegram Delivered to Philip Malloy

TO: PHILIP MALLOY

American Legion Post #16 of Newport, Rhode
Island, salutes you for your defense of American values. Fight the good fight. Thumbs-up!

9:20 A.M.

Conversation
between Dr. Albert Seymour
and Ted Griffen,
Candidate, Harrison School Board

DR. SEYMOUR: Mr. Griffen. Nice to meet you. Come right in.

MR. GRIFFEN: Thank you. Thank you very much.

DR. SEYMOUR: Get you some coffee?

MR. GRIFFEN: No, thanks.

DR. SEYMOUR: Looks like we're finally getting some decent weather.

MR. GRIFFEN: Absolutely.

DR. SEYMOUR: Look, Mr. Griffen—

MR. GRIFFEN: Call me Ted.

DR. SEYMOUR: Fine. Ted. I'm Al. Now, aside from wanting
to get to meet you, Ted . . . I've heard you speak—couple of times—was very interested in what you had to
say—I thought it would be a good idea—generally—to
meet you, and sort of, talk things over.

MR. GRIFFEN: Al, I appreciate that.

154
■

DR. SEYMOUR: Now—what we've got here—well, the media—they never pay attention to us unless something bad—

MR. GRIFFEN: Right. I never trust anything that's in print.

DR. SEYMOUR: Exactly. The bottom line. But we've got these elections coming up—budget.

MR. GRIFFEN: And the board.

DR. SEYMOUR: Exactly. I have a policy—I strongly believe in this—that I'm prepared to work with anyone who's on that board—the people's voice, that sort of thing. And we all want that same thing.

MR. GRIFFEN: Educating the kids.

DR. SEYMOUR: Exactly. We share that. But the budget thing—

MR. GRIFFEN: Have to keep costs down.

DR. SEYMOUR: Absolutely. But, Ted, I'll be frank with you. All this publicity—negative publicity—isn't—won't—do us any good.

MR. GRIFFEN: I understand.

DR. SEYMOUR: And, you understand, that first budget was tight—and this second one—to the bone. Get any closer and we're scooping marrow. And I understand—no one wants to pay a cent more. But without that budget, education is in big trouble here in Harrison.

MR. GRIFFEN: People want to hold the line on taxes.

DR. SEYMOUR: I sympathize. I pay taxes too. But—again to be frank—there's been a real misunderstanding regarding this national anthem thing. It doesn't help.

155

MR. GRIFFEN: Very disturbing.

DR. SEYMOUR: Exactly. It is. Let me share some of the facts with you.

MR. GRIFFEN: That's all I'm looking for.

DR. SEYMOUR: I appreciate that. What the media has done is confuse certain things—

MR. GRIFFEN: Something is confused.

DR. SEYMOUR: Exactly. First, though, let me tell you so you're quite clear, we have *no* rule against singing the national anthem. Never have had. Never will. Not as long as I'm superintendent.

MR. GRIFFEN: But the boy was suspended.

DR. SEYMOUR: Just getting to that. What I suspect here— we've got—a personal problem.

MR. GRIFFEN: The boy? He seems—

DR. SEYMOUR: Now, Ted, I'm speaking in confidence.

MR. GRIFFEN: Sure.

DR. SEYMOUR: Then we understand. Ted, it's not the boy. It's the teacher.

MR. GRIFFEN: This Narwin gal?

DR. SEYMOUR: Exactly.

MR. GRIFFEN: Well, I thought . . . What kind—between you and me—what kind of a problem?

DR. SEYMOUR: Okay. Let me quote from a letter she wrote—this was to her principal—just a few weeks ago—I can't give you a copy, you understand—privacy and all—

MR. GRIFFEN: I understand.

DR. SEYMOUR: But I can read a part of it to you—so you can understand what I'm up against.

MR. GRIFFEN: Sure. Go on.

DR. SEYMOUR: She says—this Narwin woman—yes, here— now, I'm quoting her. "The truth is . . . I feel that sometimes"—get this—"I am a little out of touch with contemporary teaching, and, just as important, the students who come before me." In other words, she's been around, what can I say, since history began.

MR. GRIFFEN: Oh boy. . . . You've got a problem there. Tenure.

DR. SEYMOUR: Exactly. The question is, what are you and I going to do about it?

12:30 P.M.

Lunchroom Conversation
between Philip Malloy and Todd Becker

TODD BECKER: You don't have to sit alone, you know.

PHILIP MALLOY: I'm okay.

TODD BECKER: Can I sit?

PHILIP MALLOY: Suit yourself.

TODD BECKER: What's happening?

PHILIP MALLOY: Nothing.

TODD BECKER: That true you're going to be on TV?

PHILIP MALLOY: Who told you that?

TODD BECKER: Susan Vogle.

PHILIP MALLOY: No way.

TODD BECKER: But you're famous, right? All that newspaper stuff.

PHILIP MALLOY: What you come over here for? Just to tease me?

TODD BECKER: Just trying to be friendly.

PHILIP MALLOY: Yeah. Sure. Stuff it.

TODD BECKER: Suit yourself.

157
■

Faculty Lunchroom Conversation
between Margaret Narwin and Mr. Benison

MR. BENISON: You okay, Peg?

MISS NARWIN: Bit of a headache.

MR. BENISON: I saw those telegrams.

MISS NARWIN: It's awful.

MR. BENISON: Yeah, well, it's a crazy world. Who's that guy who said everybody will be famous for a few minutes?

MISS NARWIN: Andy Warhol. I really can't stand this.

MR. BENISON: I know. Lot of people upset. That's for sure.

MISS NARWIN: What do you mean?

MR. BENISON: I must have had ten calls last night saying— neighbors, a couple of family people—asking, is it true? I told them look, it wasn't anything like that. That you didn't mean it to happen that way.

MISS NARWIN: What did you say I meant?

MR. BENISON: You know, some personal thing, happens all the time. . . .

MISS NARWIN: That's not what it was! The boy was being rude!

MR. BENISON: Okay, Peg, I know that, but no one expected, you know, all this. . . . What people are saying, we'll never get our budget.

MISS NARWIN: I really don't want to talk about it anymore.

MR. BENISON: Now wait a minute. Peg . . . don't go off. . . .

Conversation
between Philip Malloy and Margaret Narwin

PHILIP MALLOY: Miss Narwin?

MISS NARWIN: Philip? What are you doing here? What do you want?

PHILIP MALLOY: My class.

MISS NARWIN: You're . . . you're not in this section anymore. You were switched.

PHILIP MALLOY: I was?

MISS NARWIN: You're in Mr. Keegan's class.

PHILIP MALLOY: But—

MISS NARWIN: What?

PHILIP MALLOY: To get my grade up—I was going to ask for extra work. . . .

MISS NARWIN: Philip, you are no longer in my class. Didn't you hear me?

PHILIP MALLOY: So I could get on the track team and . . .

MISS NARWIN: You are not in my class.

PHILIP MALLOY: But what about the grade?

MISS NARWIN: Please leave the room. I want you out. Sara, take this note to Dr. Doane. . . .

PHILIP MALLOY: But . . .

MISS NARWIN: You must leave. Go!

PHILIP MALLOY: I'm leaving.

MISS NARWIN: Speak to Dr. Doane. Now, please, leave!

159

Conversation
between Philip Malloy and Coach Jamison

COACH JAMISON: Oh, Philip. Didn't see you there.

PHILIP MALLOY: Can I talk to you a minute?

COACH JAMISON: Yeah. Sure. Got a minute.

PHILIP MALLOY: Remember, you said I should ask Miss Narwin for some extra work. . . .

COACH JAMISON: Sure.

PHILIP MALLOY: So I could get my grade up, get on the team.

COACH JAMISON: Okay.

PHILIP MALLOY: She won't let me.

COACH JAMISON: She won't let you what?

PHILIP MALLOY: Do more work.

COACH JAMISON: Well, look, you did one hell of a number on her. . . .

PHILIP MALLOY: I mean, I'm not even in her class anymore. She must have kicked me out.

COACH JAMISON: They put you in another class?

PHILIP MALLOY: Yeah, but I was trying to get some extra work. . . . If I could stay in her class I—

COACH JAMISON: Philip, you want my advice?

160
■ PHILIP MALLOY: I tried—

COACH JAMISON: I'm always telling you guys—it's what sports is all about—a rule is a rule—to get along you have to play along. Know what I'm saying?

PHILIP MALLOY: What about my running with the team?

COACH JAMISON: Look, Philip, you did a number on Miss
  Narwin. Didn't I tell you—right from the start—you
  were way off base? She's a good person. You have to be
  a team player. Haven't you heard me say that? So you
  can't just come around now and start asking me for things.
  It just doesn't work that way. Look, Phil, I've got a practice. And look, by next year this'll all be over. I sure
  hope so.

3:30 P.M.

Conversation
between Margaret Narwin and
Dr. Gertrude Doane

DR. DOANE: Would you like a cup of coffee?

MISS NARWIN: My nerves are too tight as it is.

DR. DOANE: It's astonishing. . . . Did I tell you, I had another call from a TV reporter—

MISS NARWIN: No. Absolutely not.

DR. DOANE: I don't blame you.

MISS NARWIN: You wanted to see me. . . .

DR. DOANE: Just that some good has come out of all this. . . .

MISS NARWIN: That would be nice. What is it?

DR. DOANE: Peg, do you remember you put in an application
  for funds? Some kind of refresher course, English teaching. I'm not sure what. For the summer.

MISS NARWIN: Vaguely.

DR. DOANE: I talked to Al Seymour and—

161

MISS NARWIN: Don't mention him to me. That statement—

DR. DOANE: As a way of showing his support, he managed to find some money, and you can take that special course. . . .

MISS NARWIN: Well, that is nice.

DR. DOANE: We'll expedite the application.

MISS NARWIN: I'm very grateful.

DR. DOANE: There is only one thing. . . .

MISS NARWIN: The deadline?

DR. DOANE: No, it's not that. Peg, knowing how upsetting this all is, the superintendent wants you to take the rest of the term off.

MISS NARWIN: What?

DR. DOANE: The rest of the term.

MISS NARWIN: But . . .

DR. DOANE: Well, Al knows, because I told him, how upsetting all this is to you, and . . . Take the time off, full pay, of course, and then, take that course, and you'll come back fall term . . . and, well, things will be fine. It's very kind of him.

MISS NARWIN: In other words, he wants me to leave.

DR. DOANE: No. No. You've misunderstood. Truly, Peg. Only as a way of getting out from the pressure. I mean, all these telegrams. Calls. It would be administrative leave. You'll lose no time on your pension. As I said, full-time. With pay. You could be with your sister. . . . A sabbatical. You've never had one.

162
■

MISS NARWIN: No.

DR. DOANE: Peg, you have to see it from his, our side. . . .

MISS NARWIN: Aren't we on the same side?

DR. DOANE: That's not the point.

MISS NARWIN: What *is* the point?

DR. DOANE: Peg, Al is deeply worried about our budget.

6:30 P.M.

Conversation
between Philip Malloy's Parents

MR. MALLOY: Hey, where's Philip?

MRS. MALLOY: Up in his room.

MR. MALLOY: These telegrams. Incredible.

MRS. MALLOY: He's very upset.

MR. MALLOY: About the telegrams?

MRS. MALLOY: Something at school.

MR. MALLOY: That teacher again?

MRS. MALLOY: He wouldn't say. When he came home, I don't think he even looked at that stack. He doesn't seem very happy. He wouldn't talk about it.

MR. MALLOY: Weird.

MRS. MALLOY: I almost thought he was going to start crying.

MR. MALLOY: *Crying?*

MRS. MALLOY: Maybe you could talk to him.

MR. MALLOY: Sure.

MRS. MALLOY: Dinner will be ready in twenty minutes. 163

MR. MALLOY: I'll talk to him.

MRS. MALLOY: Hon!

MR. MALLOY: What?

MRS. MALLOY: My sister called.

MR. MALLOY: From Conover?

MRS. MALLOY: She said Philip could go to school in their district.

MR. MALLOY: That's absurd!

MRS. MALLOY: Maybe it isn't. Maybe this is too much.

MR. MALLOY: Susan . . .

MRS. MALLOY: Just a thought.

6:45 P.M.

Phone Conversation
between Margaret Narwin and Her Sister,
Anita Wigham

ANITA WIGHAM: Peg, I am shocked!

MISS NARWIN: Well, you can imagine how I felt. The dishonesty of it! And from Gertrude of all people. I still find it impossible to believe.

ANITA WIGHAM: But what are you going to do?

MISS NARWIN: Anita, I don't know. I truly don't know.

6:50 P.M.

Conversation
between Philip Malloy and His Father

MR. MALLOY: Philip, I want you to open the door so we can talk.

PHILIP MALLOY: I don't want to talk.

MR. MALLOY: What happened in school?

PHILIP MALLOY: Nothing.

MR. MALLOY: Look, dinner will be ready in five minutes.

PHILIP MALLOY: I'm not hungry.

MR. MALLOY: Then what are you going to do?

PHILIP MALLOY: I don't know.

8:30 P.M.

From a Speech
Delivered by Ted Griffen to a Meeting
of the Harrison Downtown Association

MR. CRIFFEN: That I can be a forceful, productive member
of the board is clear. It was I who made public this sad
story regarding a boy who was removed from class merely
because of his desire to express his patriotism. Even
though I am not yet a member of the board, I was able
to meet with Superintendent Seymour—who has, I assure you, my deepest respect—and discuss in a calm,
rational fashion what might be done. When it became
clear that the problem was not with school policy itself,
but the misguided judgment of a particular teacher—a
teacher out of touch with Harrison values—a solution
was worked out that is equitable to all—and preserves
the good name of our community. The boy is back in
class, where he belongs and wants to be. The teacher in
question will get a needed refresher course in our values
and return to her duties next year better able to teach.

Our community will support just these kinds of productive compromises. And therefore I urge all of you, on
April fifth, to support the school budget proposal set
before the voters. It is a thoughtful budget. Let me make

this perfectly clear. The budget is fiscally prudent, and I, for one, support it.

8:50 P.M.

From the Diary of Philip Malloy

Things stink. And it's all so unfair. Nobody takes my side. They all think Narwin's great. Nobody pays any attention to what she did to me. Coach Jamison won't let me on the team. I hate that school.

9:30 P.M.

Phone Conversation between Margaret Narwin and Robert Duval, Reporter

MISS NARWIN: I really don't wish to talk about it.

MR. DUVAL: Ma'am, Miss Narwin, it seems to me, from what I've come to understand about you and what happened, that the original story does not make a great deal of sense. For instance, at one point, Dr. Doane—your principal— told me you were one of the district's best teachers.

MISS NARWIN: Did she?

MR. DUVAL: Yes, ma'am. She did.

MISS NARWIN: I'm not so sure she would still say so.

MR. DUVAL: What do you mean?

MISS NARWIN: Mr. Duval . . . I . . .

MR. DUVAL: Miss Narwin, I am truly interested in getting out your story. It's been awfully one-sided.

MISS NARWIN: That's certainly true. People seem to believe that this boy is . . . rather special. Nobody seems to want to pay any attention to what actually happened. I've been asked to resign.

MR. DUVAL: By whom?

MISS NARWIN: The school. The district.

MR. DUVAL: Miss Narwin, I'm prepared to fly out and talk to you. I really do think there is something important here. I'd like to get it out to the public. Miss Narwin?

MISS NARWIN: Very well. Come along. I'll talk to you.

17

Wednesday, April 4

7:20 A.M.

Phone Conversation between Margaret Narwin and Dr. Gertrude Doane

DR. DOANE: Yes, Peg?

MISS NARWIN: I won't be coming in today.

DR. DOANE: Oh.

MISS NARWIN: I'm too exhausted.

DR. DOANE: I think that's wise.

MISS NARWIN: I need time to think.

DR. DOANE: You do that. No problem here. We'll get a substitute.

7:30 A.M.

Conversation between Philip Malloy and His Parents at Breakfast

168

PHILIP MALLOY: No way I'm going to school.

MR. MALLOY: Why?

PHILIP MALLOY: I just won't.

MRS. MALLOY: Philip, you must tell us. Has that teacher done something else?

PHILIP MALLOY: I'm not in her classes anymore.

MR. MALLOY: But . . . Look at all these telegrams. Everybody says you did the right thing.

PHILIP MALLOY: I'm not going.

MR. MALLOY: Philip, you must go.

PHILIP MALLOY: I'll go to another school. You said there was a private school.

MRS. MALLOY: But . . .

MR. MALLOY: Oh, sure! Go to private school! The only money we've got is the money we've been putting aside for your college.

PHILIP MALLOY: I could go up to Aunt Becky's. We could move.

MR. MALLOY: That's ridiculous. Look, it's clear *something* has happened. If we don't know, how can we help you?

PHILIP MALLOY: The kids hate me!

MR. MALLOY: Why?

PHILIP MALLOY: I'm not going.

MR. MALLOY: Philip, you will go!

7:40 A.M.

Conversation
between Philip Malloy and Ken Barchet
on the Way to the School Bus

PHILIP MALLOY: What's happening?

KEN BARCHET: Nothing. What's with you? I thought maybe you weren't going to school.

PHILIP MALLOY: My folks . . .

KEN BARCHET: Did you hear what Allison and Todd were planning to do?

PHILIP MALLOY: No, what?

KEN BARCHET: They want to get a petition going to get you to say you were wrong.

PHILIP MALLOY: No way.

KEN BARCHET: And you know who gave them the idea?

PHILIP MALLOY: No.

KEN BARCHET: Coach Jamison.

PHILIP MALLOY: You kidding?

KEN BARCHET: That's what Brian told me. Want me to start another petition to get Narwin to apologize? Or we could get you to sing together. Be boss.

PHILIP MALLOY: Would you stop bugging me!

KEN BARCHET: Hey, man, can't you take a joke?

PHILIP MALLOY: Forget it!

KEN BARCHET: Hey! Come on, Phil. Where you going? I was just kidding!

8:55 A.M.

Phone Conversation
between Philip Malloy and His Mother

170
■

PHILIP MALLOY: Just want you to know I'm home.

MRS. MALLOY: *Home?* Why?

PHILIP MALLOY: I told you: I'm not going to school. Not that school.

MRS. MALLOY. Well . . . stay home today. That's okay. We'll talk it out when I get home.

PHILIP MALLOY: Just don't tell Dad, will you?

MRS. MALLOY: Okay.

10:55 P.M.

Conversation
between Philip Malloy's Parents

MRS. MALLOY: Ben, but he refuses to go back!

MR. MALLOY: I've never heard of anything so crazy. He won! But he acts as if he's lost.

MRS. MALLOY: He says he'll just wait till we're out of the house and then come home.

MR. MALLOY: Of all . . .

MRS. MALLOY: He has to go to some school.

MR. MALLOY: Right . . .

MRS. MALLOY: I'm going to call Washington Academy.

MR. MALLOY: That's his college money!

MRS. MALLOY: Or should I call my sister?

Conversation
between Margaret Narwin
and Robert Duval, Reporter

MR. DUVAL: Miss Narwin, how do you see what has happened? A summary.

MISS NARWIN: I think and I think. And—that boy—Philip Malloy—for reasons I'll never learn—decided to insult me, his classmates, and, as far as that goes, the national anthem. Yes, I sent him from my room. But it wasn't I who sent him home. I objected to that. Objected strongly. Yet I've been blamed for his suspension. It's I who has been asked to resign.

MR. DUVAL: Resign?

MISS NARWIN: They say it's a leave. But Mr. Duval, I'm not stupid. Naïve perhaps. But not stupid. I should be in school right this moment, teaching my students. Teaching them the literature that I love. That they desperately need. Who else will give it to them? But where am I? I'm home—surrounded by letters, and telegrams too— from people, perfect strangers who know nothing about me, who hate me. The post office brought a sack of letters this morning. That's why I'm talking to you. I'm trying to defend myself.

Mr. Duval, as I see it, I have been working—working hard—as a teacher for twenty years. I've been a good teacher. Ask my principal if that's not so. Do you know, she was once my student.

172

MR. DUVAL: Is that right?

MISS NARWIN: Oh, yes. One of the brightest. But did *anyone*—anyone outside—ever stop and notice those years of good teaching—did they write a story about *that*? No.

That's not what people are interested in. Do you know—
I feel like I've been mugged. Assaulted.

MR. DUVAL: By whom?

MISS NARWIN: I wish I knew.

MR. DUVAL: Ma'am, do you think there's some reason that
this has happened?

MISS NARWIN: Reason? Mr. Duval, I keep wishing there was
a reason. No, no reason at all.

MR. DUVAL: Do you have any idea what you will do about
it?

MISS NARWIN: I told you, I'm thinking of resigning.

18

Friday, April 6

Report from the *Manchester Record* on School Elections

HARRISON SCHOOL ELECTIONS

Final results, vote for school budget:
In Favor: 645
Against: 1,784
Budget Defeated

The following were elected to the Harrison
School Board for three-year terms:
Susan Eagleton
Ted Griffen
Gloria Haviland
Ernest Johnson
Crawford Wright

Percentage of eligible voters casting ballots:
22%

10:25 A.M.

Conversation
between Margaret Narwin
and Robert Duval, Reporter

---

174   MISS NARWIN: Mr. Duval?

MR. DUVAL: Speaking.

MISS NARWIN: This is Margaret Narwin, from Harrison.

MR. DUVAL: Oh, yes, Miss Narwin. How are you, ma'am?

MISS NARWIN: I'm fine. I wanted to ask you if you published that story—that story that you interviewed me for.

MR. DUVAL: Oh, right. Well, I certainly wrote it. And it has been filed. It was a pretty good story. All set to go too. But then South America . . . that situation . . . There's no room.

MISS NARWIN: Then you won't print it?

MR. DUVAL: Well, it's possible. But I'd be less than candid with you if I said it will appear. With so much happening . . .

MISS NARWIN: I see.

MR. DUVAL: I am sorry. I'm sure you would have liked to see it in print. . . .

MISS NARWIN: Yes. . . .

MR. DUVAL: Did you decide what to do, ma'am?

MISS NARWIN: I'm . . . I'm calling from the airport now. I'm going to Florida. To be with my sister. And her husband.

MR. DUVAL: You've resigned, then.

MISS NARWIN: I need some time to think. . . .

MR. DUVAL: Yes, I understand. And I—excuse me, I'm being called. . . .

19

Monday, April 9

8:25 A.M.

Conversation
between Philip Malloy
and George Brookover,
Principal of Washington Academy

GEORGE BROOKOVER: Philip, I just want to tell you that we're very pleased to have you at Washington Academy. We do know a good bit about you. You're pretty famous.

PHILIP MALLOY: Yes, sir.

GEORGE BROOKOVER: We like what we hear. Anyway, we're all pretty much a family at Washington. I'm sure you'll make new friends.

PHILIP MALLOY: Yes, sir.

GEORGE BROOKOVER: You'll be in Miss Rooney's class. You'll find her a good teacher. I'm sure you'll do just fine. Have you any interest in sports?

PHILIP MALLOY: Track.

GEORGE BROOKOVER: Well, we don't have a track team here at Washington. There's never been enough interest. But now that you're here, maybe there can be. Your dad says you're a crackerjack runner. We do have soccer. You could do a lot of running there. Think that might interest you?

176
■

PHILIP MALLOY: I don't know.

GEORGE BROOKOVER: Okay. Let me take you on down to class now. Should be just getting under way.

Discussion
in Miss Rooney's Homeroom Class,
Washington Academy

MISS ROONEY: Class, this is Philip Malloy, who has just joined our school. Philip, you can sit right over there. We were about to begin. In fact, we usually begin by singing the national anthem. Maybe you'd like to lead us in that? Philip? Philip, what's the matter? Why are you crying?

PHILIP MALLOY: I don't know the words.

CONNECTIONS

Did you know that Avi got the idea for Nothing but the Truth from a type of play that was performed in the 1930s? It seems only natural, then, for Avi's novel to be turned into a play. As you read the first part of the play, imagine watching it on a stage. How does it get your attention? How does it make you think about Philip's story?

Nothing but the Truth: A Play

an excerpt from the play (an adaptation of Avi's novel)

Ronn Smith

PROLOG

Spot up on PHILIP MALLOY, who is standing in the DC acting area.

PHILIP MALLOY (*to the audience*): Two questions. Do you swear to tell the truth, the whole truth, and nothing but the truth? (*pause*) Does anyone ever say no?

Blackout.

SCENE ONE

SLIDE: *"Tuesday, March 13. 10:35 P.M. From the Diary of Philip Malloy"*

Lights up on PHILIP MALLOY, standing in the DC acting area. He is holding his diary.

PHILIP MALLOY (*to the audience*): Coach Jamison stopped me in the hall today to say that I should try out for the track team! That with me on the Harrison High team we could be county champs. Fantastic! He wouldn't say that unless he meant it. Will have to ask the folks to help me get new shoes. But Dad was so excited I'm sure he'll help. (*He begins to leave, but then stops and turns back to the audience.*)
    Oh, yeah. Sarah Gloss came over at lunch to say this girl, Allison Doresett, likes me. I wasn't sure who Allison was. Then I remembered.

She's in my English class. Bet she heard about my running. Girls like guys who win. Ta-da! It's Malloy Magic time!

Talk about Malloy Magic. This time for—da-dum!—Miss Narwin. I mean, what can you do with an English teacher who's so uptight she must have been put together with superglue. She won't let people have their own minds about anything! And the stuff she makes us read! I can't believe how *boring* Jack London is! *The Call of the Wild.* Talk about dogs! Ma says *she* had to read it in school. There has to be better stuff to read. I thought high school was going to be different. *(beat)* Have to figure out a way to run past Narwin.

SLIDE: "*10:45 P.M. From a Letter Written by Margaret Narwin to Her Sister, Anita Wigham*"

PHILIP MALLOY exits and MARGARET NARWIN, holding the letter, enters. She stops in the DC acting area.

MARGARET NARWIN (*to the audience*): Yes, a body gets a little tired after doing *anything* for twenty-one years. And I have been teaching at Harrison High for that long. But I still believe I was meant to bring fine literature to young minds. When the connection is made—and from time to time it *is* made—it's all worth it. The truth is, I like my work. (*beat*)

But the other truth, Anita, is that students today are not what they used to be. There is no love of literature. They come to it reluctantly, fighting every inch of the way. I like them and their capacity for independence, but they seem to lack caring for anything other than themselves. If they ask me once more "What's this have to do with *us*?" I think I'll scream.

For example, right now I'm teaching *The Call of the Wild.* This boy, Philip Malloy, raised his hand to say he didn't understand "who was calling who." Now if I were to laugh, he would have been insulted. And I would have lost him. You have to treat students with such care and fairness.

This Philip is only a middling student, which is a shame. He's a nice-looking boy. Intelligent. With real potential. Perhaps that's why he irritates me so, for he shows no desire to strive, to make sacrifices for the betterment of himself. Like so many students, he exhibits *no* desire to learn. But it's not even *that* that I mind so much. It's a certain something—a resistance—to the idea that literature is important. But it is. I know it is. If I could only convince students of this.

I can hear you saying, "Come down to Florida." Anita, I don't know if I am ready. Yes, I could take early retirement, but the truth is, I would be lost without my books, my teaching, my students.

SCENE TWO

SLIDE: *"Thursday, March 15. 8:05 A.M. Bernard Lunser's Homeroom Class"*

> *PHILIP MALLOY, STUDENT #1, STUDENT #2, STUDENT #3,*
> *and BERNARD LUNSER in SL acting area. General commotion.*
> *SLIDE (on rear projection screen behind SL area): Classroom*
> *wall, maybe a blackboard or a row of windows.*

BERNARD LUNSER: Let's go! Let's go! Time to grab the moment!

INTERCOM *(voice of DR. GERTRUDE DOANE)*: Good morning to all students, faculty, and staff. Today is Thursday, March fifteenth. Today will be a Schedule A day.

BERNARD LUNSER: Get that, bozos? *A* day!

INTERCOM: Today in history. On this day in forty-four B.C., Julius Caesar was assassinated.

BERNARD LUNSER: And right after that they all ate a Caesar salad.

INTERCOM: It was in eighteen-twenty that Maine was admitted to the United States.

BERNARD LUNSER: And by eighteen-twenty-one they wanted out.

INTERCOM: Please all rise and stand at respectful, silent attention for the playing of our national anthem.

> *PHILIP MALLOY and the other STUDENTS stand. PHILIP MALLOY's attention is on the book lying open on his desk as the first verse of The Star-Spangled Banner is played over the intercom. (In following scenes, unless otherwise noted, fade out music soon after the dialogue has been concluded.)*

Oh, say, can you see by the dawn's early light,
What so proudly we hailed at the twilight's last gleaming? . . .

BERNARD LUNSER: Okay, Philip, is that your homework you're working on?

Whose broad stripes and bright stars, thro' the perilous fight . . .

PHILIP MALLOY: I'm trying to pass an exam.

BERNARD LUNSER: Ah, the famous wit and wisdom of Mr. Malloy. Put the book away.

■ ■ ■

The national anthem plays an important role in Nothing but the Truth. *The anthem itself was born out of conflict—the War of 1812. Read on to learn more about how the song came to be written; then, read the complete lyrics.*

The Star-Spangled Banner

from The American Flag

Thomas Parrish

It was a foggy, drizzly night in mid-September 1814. A little sloop named the *Minden* lay quietly in the waters of Chesapeake Bay, near Baltimore. In front of the *Minden* a line of sixteen British ships fired cannons and rockets into the mist. On the deck of the little ship a man paced back and forth, watching the mighty bombardment. This man was a thirty-five-year-old Washington lawyer and amateur poet named Francis Scott Key.

He was not a participant in the fighting. Nor was he on board the *Minden* because he liked to watch bombardments. He was acting as a diplomat, a person who negotiates with representatives of foreign countries. He was doing this to help a friend and neighbor, an elderly doctor named William Beanes. Dr. Beanes was a prisoner of war. His captors were the British, who for two years had been engaged in a new war with the United States. They had landed five thousand troops at Washington and burned the Capitol and the White House. They had next planned to take Baltimore. The British fleet was supposed to help the land forces by attacking and knocking out Fort McHenry, which defended Baltimore against attack by sea.

The British general had apparently been in an optimistic mood that morning. He is supposed to have said, "I will have supper in Baltimore or in Hell." Neither he nor any other British soldier had supper in Baltimore that night. The general himself had been killed in the land attack, which was thrown back by the militiamen defending the town. The army of the British had failed. Everything now depended on their fleet.

Francis Scott Key had not expected to spend that night in the midst of a bombardment. With another American negotiator, he had come out to the British fleet during the preceding day. Their aim was to ask the British admiral to release Dr. Beanes. After some strong argument, the admiral had agreed: Dr. Beanes was an old man, and perhaps he had been wrongly taken prisoner. But during the day the two Americans had heard the British officers discussing their plans to attack Fort McHenry. The admiral had therefore told them that they could return to the *Minden* but must stay behind the British lines until the battle was over.

Fort McHenry was only a small fortification, not a great citadel. Its chances of surviving a battering from sixteen heavy ships of the British navy did not seem very strong. But as the hours went by, it continued to return the British fire. Then the barrage stopped. Why? Had the British given up the attack? Or had the bombarded fort surrendered? Through the dark and the mist it was impossible to tell.

Then came day—"the dawn's early light." And there, still waving, was the "star-spangled banner." Key was overjoyed. This was one occasion he *must* honor in a poem! As he was rowed ashore, he was writing swiftly on the back of an envelope. Later that same day he finished a final draft. And within the next few days his poem was printed and distributed. It was recited in the theater and even sung. It was called "The Defence of Fort McHenry." Everybody in Baltimore seemed to know it.

Key had written a poem, not a musical composition. But his words were quickly fitted to a tune that had long been familiar in America and Britain. It was, in fact, a tune that had been used earlier for another poem of Key's. This melody was usually known by the strange-sounding name "To Anacreon in Heaven," because an English poem with that title had been sung to it. Today very few persons remember either that name or the title that Key originally gave to his poem. The words and the music long ago blended into "The Star-Spangled Banner." Strangely, although "The Star-Spangled Banner" came to be regarded as the national anthem of the United States during the nineteenth century, it was not officially adopted until 1931.

The Star-Spangled Banner
Francis Scott Key

Oh, say can you see by the dawn's early light
What so proudly we hail'd at the twilight's last gleaming
Whose broad stripes and bright stars through the perilous fight
O'er the ramparts we watch'd were so gallantly streaming?
And the rockets' red glare the bombs bursting in air,
Gave proof through the night that our flag was still there.
Oh, say does that star-spangled banner yet wave
O'er the land of the free and the home of the brave?

On the shore dimly seen through the mists of the deep,
Where the foe's haughty host in the dread silence reposes,
What is that which the breeze, o'er the towering steep,
As it fitfully blows, half conceals, half discloses?
Now it catches the gleam of the morning's first beam,
In full glory reflected now shines in the stream.
'Tis the star-spangled banner, oh, long may it wave
O'er the land of the free and the home of the brave!

And where is that band who so vauntingly swore
That the havoc of war and the battle's confusion
A home and a country should leave us no more?
Their blood has wash'd out their foul footstep's pollution.
No refuge could save the hireling and slave
From the terror of flight or the gloom of the grave,
And the star-spangled banner in triumph doth wave
O'er the land of the free and the home of the brave.

Oh, thus be it ever when freemen shall stand
Between their lov'd home and the war's desolation!
Blest with vict'ry and peace may the heav'n-rescued land
Praise the power that hath made and preserv'd us a nation!
Then conquer we must, when our cause it is just,
And this be our motto, In God Is Our Trust,
And the star-spangled banner in triumph shall wave
O'er the land of the free and the home of the brave.

■ ■ ■

*"Unfair!" That's the way Philip feels about his treatment at school. In this
story, another student feels the same way, but for entirely different reasons.
As you read, remember one of Philip's comments: "But everybody says I was
right. And I was." Do you think Philip would believe the narrator of this story
is right?*

The Revolt of the Evil Fairies
Ted Poston

The grand dramatic offering of the Booker T. Washington Colored
Grammar School was the biggest event of the year in our social life in
Hopkinsville, Kentucky. It was the one occasion on which they let us
use the old Cooper Opera House, and even some of the white folks
came out yearly to applaud our presentation. The first two rows of the
orchestra were always reserved for our white friends, and our leading
colored citizens sat right behind them—with an empty row intervening,
of course.

Mr. Ed Smith, our local undertaker, invariably occupied a box to the
left of the house and wore his cutaway coat and striped breeches. This
distinctive garb was usually reserved for those rare occasions when he
officiated at the funerals of our most prominent colored citizens. Mr.
Thaddeus Long, our colored mailman, once rented a tuxedo and bought
a box too. But nobody paid him much mind. We knew he was just
showing off.

The title of our play never varied. It was always Prince Charming and
the Sleeping Beauty, but no two presentations were ever the same. Miss
H. Belle LaPrade, our sixth-grade teacher, rewrote the script every season,
and it was never like anything you read in the storybooks.

Miss LaPrade called it "a modern morality play of conflict between
the forces of good and evil." And the forces of evil, of course, always
came off second best.

The Booker T. Washington Colored Grammar School was in a state of
ferment from Christmas until February, for this was the period when
parts were assigned. First there was the selection of the Good Fairies and

the Evil Fairies. This was very important, because the Good Fairies wore white costumes and the Evil Fairies black. And strangely enough most of the Good Fairies usually turned out to be extremely light in complexion, with straight hair and white folks' features. On rare occasions a dark-skinned girl might be lucky enough to be a Good Fairy, but not one with a speaking part.

There never was any doubt about Prince Charming and the Sleeping Beauty. They were always lightskinned. And though nobody ever discussed those things openly, it was an accepted fact that a lack of pigmentation was a decided advantage in the Prince Charming and Sleeping Beauty sweepstakes.

And therein lay my personal tragedy. I made the best grades in my class, I was the leading debater, and the scion of a respected family in the community. But I could never be Prince Charming, because I was black.

In fact, every year when they started casting our grand dramatic offering my family started pricing black cheesecloth at Franklin's Department Store. For they knew that I would be leading the forces of darkness and skulking back in the shadows—waiting to be vanquished in the third act. Mamma had experience with this sort of thing. All my brothers had finished Booker T. before me.

Not that I was alone in my disappointment. Many of my classmates felt it too. I probably just took it more to heart. Rat Joiner for instance, could rationalize the situation. Rat was not only black; he lived on Billy Goat Hill. But Rat summed it up like this:

"If you black, you black."

I should have been able to regard the matter calmly too. For our grand dramatic offering was only a reflection of our daily community life in Hopkinsville. The yallers had the best of everything. They held most of the teaching jobs in Booker T. Washington Colored Grammar School. They were the Negro doctors, the lawyers, the insurance men. They even had a "Blue Vein Society," and if your dark skin obscured your throbbing pulse you were hardly a member of the elite.

Yet I was inconsolable the first time they turned me down for Prince Charming. That was the year they picked Roger Jackson. Roger was not only dumb; he stuttered. But he was light enough to pass for white, and that was apparently sufficient.

In all fairness, however, it must be admitted that Roger had other qualifications. His father owned the only colored saloon in town and was quite a power in local politics. In fact, Mr. Clinton Jackson had a lot to say about just who taught in the Booker T. Washington Colored Grammar School. So it was understandable that Roger should have been picked for Prince Charming.

My real heartbreak, however, came the year they picked Sarah Williams for Sleeping Beauty. I had been in love with Sarah since kindergarten. She had soft light hair, bluish-gray eyes, and a dimple which stayed in her left cheek whether she was smiling or not.

Of course Sarah never encouraged me much. She never answered any of my fervent love letters, and Rat was very scornful of my one-sided love affairs. "As long as she don't call you a black baboon," he sneered, "you'll keep on hanging around."

After Sarah was chosen for Sleeping Beauty, I went out for the Prince Charming role with all my heart. If I had declaimed boldly in previous contests, I was matchless now. If I had bothered Mamma with rehearsals at home before, I pestered her to death this time. Yes, and I purloined my sister's can of Palmer's Skin Success.

I knew the Prince's role from start to finish, having played the Head Evil Fairy opposite it for two seasons. And Prince Charming was one character whose lines Miss LaPrade never varied much in her many versions. But although I never admitted it, even to myself, I knew I was doomed from the start. They gave the part to Leonardius Wright. Leonardius, of course, was yarrler.

The teachers sensed my resentment. They were almost apologetic. They pointed out that I had been such a splendid Head Evil Fairy for two seasons that it would be a crime to let anybody else try the role. They reminded me that Mamma wouldn't have to buy any more cheesecloth because I could use my same old costume. They insisted that the Head Evil Fairy was even more important than Prince Charming because he was the one who cast the spell on Sleeping Beauty. So what could I do but accept?

I had never liked Leonardius Wright. He was a goody-goody, and even Mamma was always throwing him up to me. But, above all, he too was in love with Sarah Williams. And now he got a chance to kiss Sarah every day in rehearsing the awakening scene.

Well, the show must go on, even for little black boys. So I threw my soul into my part and made the Head Evil Fairy a character to be remembered. When I drew back from the couch of Sleeping Beauty and slunk away into the shadows at the approach of Prince Charming, my facial expression was indeed something to behold. When I was vanquished by the shining sword of Prince Charming in the last act, I was a little hammy perhaps—but terrific!

The attendance at our grand dramatic offering that year was the best in its history. Even the white folks overflowed the two rows reserved for them, and a few were forced to sit in the intervening one. This created a delicate situation, but everybody tactfully ignored it.

When the curtain went up on the last act, the audience was in fine fettle. Everything had gone well for me too—except for one spot in the second act. That was where Leonardius unexpectedly rapped me over the head with his sword as I slunk off into the shadows. That was not in the script, but Miss LaPrade quieted me down by saying it made a nice touch anyway. Rat said Leonardius did it on purpose.

The third act went on smoothly, though, until we came to the vanquishing scene. That was where I slunk from the shadows for the last time and challenged Prince Charming to mortal combat. The hero reached for his shining sword—a bit unsportsmanlike, I always thought, since Miss LaPrade consistently left the Head Evil Fairy unarmed—and then it happened!

Later I protested loudly—but in vain—that it was a case of self-defense. I pointed out that Leonardius had a mean look in his eye. I cited the impromptu rapping he had given my head in the second act. But nobody would listen. They just wouldn't believe that Leonardius really intended to brain me when he reached for his sword.

Anyway, he didn't succeed. For the minute I saw that evil gleam in his eye—or was it my own?—I cut loose with a right to the chin, and Prince Charming dropped his shining sword and staggered back. His astonishment lasted only a minute, though, for he lowered his head and came charging in, fists flailing. There was nothing yellow about Leonardius but his skin.

The audience thought the scrap was something new Miss LaPrade had written in. They might have kept on thinking so if Miss LaPrade hadn't been screaming so hysterically from the sidelines. And if Rat Joiner hadn't decided that this was as good a time as any to settle old scores. So he turned around and took a sock at the male Good Fairy nearest him.

When the curtain rang down, the forces of Good and Evil were locked in combat. And Sleeping Beauty was wide awake and streaking for the wings.

They ran the curtain back up fifteen minutes later, and we finished the play. I lay down and expired according to specifications but Prince Charming will probably remember my sneering corpse to his dying day. They wouldn't let me appear in the grand dramatic offering at all the next year. But I didn't care. I couldn't have been Prince Charming anyway.

■ ■ ■

Spiking, leaping, punching—no, it's not a fight; it's a volleyball game!
During the game in this true story, Jana Benally faces a challenge that is
even more powerful than the opposing players. Read on to learn about that
challenge. Think about what the words "nothing but the truth" might mean
to Jana—and to you.

The Courage of Jana Benally
from What Do You Stand For?
Barbara A. Lewis

Jana Benally grew to be five feet eleven inches—a tall Navajo—and a star
on her high school volleyball team in Blanding, Utah. She spiked, blocked,
and scooped up impossible smashes from the other team before they hit the
floor. Her team members trusted her skills and depended upon her honesty.

But Jana hadn't always been completely honest. When she was in
fourth grade, she lied to her teacher when he asked her if she were chewing
gum. "I quickly swallowed the gum and said 'No,'" Jana remembers. "The
dumb thing about it was that I didn't need to lie. He probably would have
just asked me to spit it out. I felt so guilty, I couldn't think about anything
else, and I vowed I would never lie again."

But she did lie again, and she cheated, too. "In fifth grade, my friends
and I had a huge social studies assignment. We were all good students and
liked to finish our assignments ahead of time. So we divided up the parts
and copied from each other." Then her teacher, who conducted secret raids
on her students' desks, found three of their notebooks in one desk, all with
the same answers. The teacher called in the girls and their parents for a talk.

When Jana and her parents went to see her teacher, Jana's stomach
dropped, and all she could see were her teacher's big, round, horrified eyes,
with eyelashes that poked straight up as if they were drawn on her eyelids.
Jana burst into tears and confessed. This time, she promised herself that she
would never cheat again—or lie. For real.

And she didn't, even under pressure. Tremendous pressure. When she
was a sophomore at San Juan High School, her team played Morgan High
School in the state volleyball championship. The game was tight. Morgan

would score, then San Juan would score. Jana leaped, dove, smashed the ball, and wiped the sweat from her forehead between plays.

Near the end of the game, the score was 12 to 14, with Morgan ahead. Morgan only needed one more point to win the state championship. Morgan served to San Juan, and Jana's team passed the ball to the center. Jana set it up and spiked it down hard on Morgan's side of the net. A Morgan player dove for the ball and miraculously dug it up from the back row. The Morgan setter went underneath it and set the ball up to the off-hand hitter, who spiked it to San Juan. Jana blocked the ball and it smashed down, inbounds, on Morgan's side.

The referee blew his whistle and yelled "Side out!" San Juan got the ball, and Jana knew that her team could tie the game and maybe even win. But there was just one problem. As Jana had blocked the spike from Morgan, she had felt the underside of her arm brush the net. The referee hadn't seen it. Nobody knew but Jana.

She hesitated for a moment. Then she grabbed the net, motioned to the referee, and said "I touched the net."

Jana's coach glowered and shouted at her. "Let the ref call the game!"

The referee called "Time out!" As he studied Jana's face, his eyes widened into circles. He paused. Then he blew the whistle, called the net ball, and gave the point to Morgan.

Jana took a long, scorching shower before she left the locker room. It was quiet. Her shoes squeaked as she crossed the empty gym floor. No one on her team had blamed her—but they hadn't congratulated her for being honest, either. No one had said much of anything to Jana after the game. But she knew that it took a whole team to win or lose, and she didn't blame herself, either. Although the state championship was blown away, Jana smiled, because inside she knew she had really won.

■ ■ ■

Have you ever had one of those days when things go wrong and you just want to be left alone? Philip Malloy would understand. So would Kate Bloomfield. As you read about Kate, think about the truths in her life.

Kate Bloomfield Rebels
Jean Little

Today

Today I will not live up to my potential.

Today I will not relate well to my peer group.

Today I will not contribute in class.

    I will not volunteer one thing.

Today I will not strive to do better.

Today I will not achieve or adjust or grow enriched or get involved.

I will not put up my hand even if the teacher is wrong and I can prove it.

Today I might eat the eraser off my pencil.

I'll look at clouds.

I'll be late.

I don't think I'll wash.

I need a rest.

Mr. Entwhistle

Mr. Entwhistle was our substitute teacher. He had big shoulders and a mean mouth. He knew, before he'd laid eyes on us, that we were out to make trouble. And he knew how to handle teenagers. Step on them hard, right from the start, and you'd have no discipline problems. He'd show us who was boss the first time one of us stepped out of line.

    Looking back, I can see that was how it started. But at the time, I had not gotten around to noticing him, except to see that he was young. That's a nice change, I thought, and went back to attempting to show Sandra Mayhew where she'd fouled up in the Math homework.

Mr. Entwhistle had started writing our names in on a seating plan. He knew all the tricks. He wasn't going to put up with desk jumpers.

"What's your name?" he asked sharply.

I didn't look up, let alone answer. Sandra was finally catching on. It never once crossed my mind that he was speaking to me.

"I said 'What is your name?'" he blasted, making a real production out of it. He was closer to me. He had started down our aisle. So I glanced up. I still had not realized that I was the one he was addressing. I sat there, gazing at him, wondering why he was all charged up. I did not tell him my name.

"All right. That does it!" he thundered. "You can go to the Office."

"Me?" I said in blank amazement.

I was bewildered. Yet he was glaring straight at me. His eyes were greenish with brown speckles. They seemed to be on the point of falling out. He was absolutely frantic.

"Yes, you. Oh, yes indeed, you! Perhaps next time you'll show respect," he babbled, sidestepping to his desk like a giant crab and scribbling a note for me to take. I couldn't see what he wrote but Pete Evans told me later that it was something about insubordination. I did see that his hand was shaking. I sat there, stunned. I honestly believed that, any minute now, I'd wake up.

"On your feet!" Mr. Entwhistle shrieked. Maybe it only sounded like a shriek to me. But his voice did seem to get louder every time he spoke.

I stood up slowly. Outside the window, the sun was shining. Everything was green, beguiling. "Come," it said to me. "Just come out and away." I considered it.

At the selfsame instant, some other part of me shouted, as angrily as Mr. Entwhistle could have done, "Fight back, Kate. The bell hasn't gone. You have your rights. The others will back you up. Fight!"

Then our eyes met and I saw that he was afraid. He was just a person. He had made a mistake and now, too late, he knew it. He'd rage and bluster if I stood up to him. He'd have to. All the same, he was wishing he could go back and start over. I've felt like that.

"Yes, sir," I said quietly, and reached out my hand for the note. Nobody moved. Nobody breathed even. I was waiting for him to hand it to me; the rest of the kids, maybe, for me to start an argument. I often do. Mr. Entwhistle . . . who knows?

Then it was as though someone said, "Will the real Mr. Entwhistle please stand up?" The bombast went out of him. For one more moment, he hesitated.

"Never mind," he blurted then. "Sit down. We'll let it pass this time."

He tore the note in half, crumpled it up, and threw it at the wastebasket. Even though he missed and the wad of paper landed on the floor, even though I'd won in some way, and he'd had to back down, he looked taller.

Taking my seat I felt a bit taller myself. I shoved my hands out of sight when I saw that they were trembling. Sunlight flooded the room.

"Way to go, Kate!" Sandra cheered in a too-loud whisper. I scowled at her.

"Shh," I said.

■ ■ ■

Once a reporter learns Philip's story, things start to go crazy. It makes you think about exactly what a reporter is supposed to do. In this essay, journalist Anna Quindlen considers her job. "I am proud of what I do," she says, "and I am ashamed of it, too." See if you can figure out why.

Making News
Anna Quindlen

For most of my adult life, I have been an emotional hit-and-run driver—that is, a reporter. I made people like me, trust me, open their hearts and their minds to me, and cry and bleed onto the pages of my neat little notebooks, and then I went back to a safe place and made a story out of it. I am good at what I do, so often the people who read those stories cried, too. When they were done, they turned the page; when I was done, I went on to another person, another story—went from the cop's wife whose husband had never come home to the impoverished eighty-year-old Holocaust survivor to the family with the missing child. I stepped in and out of their lives as easily as I did into a pair of shoes in the morning, and when I was done I wrote my piece and went home, to the husband who had not been killed, the bank account that was full, the child safe in his high chair. Sometimes I carried within me, for a day or a week or perhaps even longer, the resonances of their pain. But they were left with the pain itself.

It was not always as bad as I've made it sound. On occasion I covered people who wanted to be covered and wrote about things that were not arrows to the heart: pothole programs, town meetings, the cost of living, the GNP. But I was good at something called human interest reporting, just at the time that human interest reporting became the vogue, and so I have spent a good deal of time in the homes of vulnerable strangers, setting up a short-term relationship, making them one-shot friends.

While they were lowering their defenses, I was maintaining my objectivity, which made it possible for me, in a kind of shorthand reminiscent of the "if u cn rd ths" ads on the subway, to put down in my notebook observations like "strokes baby's head and starts to cry" or "removes pictures of parents from drawer and tells how they were killed by SS."

I am proud of what I do, and I am ashamed of it, too. I am reasonably sensitive and not too ruthless, and so I have sometimes saved people from their own revelations and sometimes helped them by giving them the feeling that they were talking to someone who thought they were unique. I have never really understood why they talked to me. I am in one of the few businesses in which a service is provided, not to the people we deal with directly, but only to the faceless thousands who read about them. Sometimes reporters call our house to talk to my husband, who has tried newsworthy cases, and I do not miss the irony of the fact that I find them more or less a nuisance, depending on whether they call in the middle of dinner and how officious they are about the absolute necessity of their task.

Some people I have interviewed told me they thought they could help others know they were not alone, and I suspect they were right, and some people said they thought publicity might help them, and they were right, too. Occasionally I would write a story about a person in a bad spot and I would get checks for them in the mail, and I'd pass them along and think, "Well, that's good." But that wasn't why I did the stories. I did them for me. . . .

I know there are good reasons to do what I do. The more we understand worlds outside our own orbit, the better off we will be. I know there are people who do not believe reporters feel any of these things, that we file our feelings with the clippings, that both are soon dried out beyond saving. That's not true. The problem is that some time ago we invented a kind of new journalism and then tried to play it with old journalism rules. We approached a rape victim with the same feelings about objectivity and distance that we had brought to a press conference, and that was not fair—not so much to the rape victim, but to ourselves.

Some years ago I did a story about Stan and Julie Patz. Their names are probably familiar; their son, Etan, age six, disappeared in 1979, and they have opened their door to reporter after reporter because anything might bring him home. I interviewed Julie several years after he had gone, and at some point during our conversation my eyes filled and tears began. I thought I felt her pain—now that I have children of my own, I realize I hadn't a clue to what her pain was—but I was also angry at myself for being, after years of practice and journalism review articles, so unprofessional. I thought that what was the right response for a human being was the wrong response for a reporter.

Years have passed, and Julie's son is still missing. In the meantime, I have had two sons of my own. For a while I looked for Etan's face in every playground and schoolyard, but then I stopped. I am ashamed of that. I am proud of the story I wrote. I had the story, and Julie had the life. I still think of her sometimes, and of her pain. Now that I work as a reporter less, I am capable of bringing my emotions to it more.

Perhaps there are no unwritten rules that say you are not to feel these things. Perhaps I made them up out of my own insecurities and stereotypes, the way I insisted on drinking Scotch shots when I first got into the newspaper business, so that everyone would know I was serious stuff, not just a kid. Some of this is changing for the better, I think. The day the space shuttle exploded, at the end of the evening news, it looked to me as if Dan Rather was trembling on the verge of tears when he signed off. For a moment I was able to forget the cameras hovering over the faces of Christa McAuliffe's parents as they looked up to see their eldest child blown to bits, and to forget that if I were still in the newspaper business I might have been there too, scribbling, "Mother lays head on father's shoulder." It appeared that his emotions and his profession were merging, and it made me feel a little better about myself. But the part of me that still looks at every disaster as a story wondered for just a moment if his contact lenses were bothering him, or if the light was in his eyes.

■ ■ ■

Troubles at home, troubles at school—being a teenager isn't always easy. Philip knows it; so do you. In this story, you will see that Jeanie knows it, too. Decide whether Jeanie and Philip would see eye to eye about what truth really means.

Beauty Is Truth
Anna Guest

At 125th Street, they all got off, Jeanie and her friend, Barbara, and a crowd of other boys and girls who went to the same downtown high school. Through the train window, Jeanie thought she saw the remaining passengers look at them with relief and disdain. Around her, the boys and girls pressed forward with noisy gaiety. They were all friends now. They were home again in Harlem.

A tall boy detached himself from a group, bowed low, and swept his cap before him in a courtly salute.

"Greetings, Lady Jeanie. Greetings, Barbara."

Jeanie bit her lip. Frowning, she pulled her coat closer and shrugged. Barbara smiled and dimpled, pleased for her friend.

"I told you he likes you," she whispered. "Look, he's waiting. Want me to go on ahead?"

Jeanie really was wasting an opportunity. Norman was keen. She saw Jeanie's head, slightly bowed and thrust forward. It was no use. She was an odd girl, but Barbara liked her anyway. The boy swung gracefully back to his group.

"Coming to the show tonight?" Barbara asked.

"No, I can't. I'm so far behind in my homework, I'd better try to do some before they decide to throw me out." Jeanie still frowned.

"Want a Coke or something?" asked Barbara as they passed the big ice-cream parlor window, cluttered with candy boxes and ornate with curly lettering. They could see the juke box near the door and some boys and girls sitting down at a table. It looked warm and friendly.

Jeanie shook her head, one brief shake.

"I think I'll stop in. I'm awful thirsty," said Barbara.

Jeanie shrugged.

"So long then."

"So long."

She walked along the busy street, aimlessly looking in the store windows, turned the corner, and walked the few blocks to her house. Though it was chilly, each brownstone or gray stoop had its cluster of people clinging to the iron railings. Some children on skates played a desperate game of hockey with sticks that were not hockey sticks.

When a car approached, they did not interrupt their game until it was almost too late. Amid shouts from the driver and wild jeers from the children, the car passed, and the game was resumed in all its concentrated intensity.

Her little brother Billy was playing in front of the stoop with three or four other kids. They were bending over something on the sidewalk, in a closed circle. Pitching pennies again, she thought with repugnance. She was going to pass them, and started up the three stone steps to the doorway. A window on the ground floor opened, and Fat Mary leaned out, dressed only in a slip and a worn brown sweater.

"Now you're going to catch it, Billy Boy. Your sister's going to tell you mama you been pitching pennies again."

Jeanie did not pause.

Billy sprang up, "Hi, Jeanie. Jeanie, gimme a nickel. I need a nickel. A nickel, a nickel. I gotta have a nickel."

The other little boys took up the chant. "A nickel, a nickel. Billy needs a nickel."

She threw them a furious glance and went in. Two little girls sat on the second landing, playing house. They had a set of toy dishes spread out on the top stair, and held dolls in their laps. She stepped over them, careful not to disturb their arrangements.

The kitchen smelled dank and unused, and the opening of the door dislodged a flake of green-painted plaster. It fell into the sink, with a dry powdering. A black dress someone had given her mother lay over the chair before the sewing machine. It reminded her that her sleeve had torn half out, dressing after gym. She really should sew it, but the sight of the black dress waiting to be made over made her dislike the thought of sewing. She would just have to wear her coat in school tomorrow. Lots of kids did.

She hung her coat on a hook in the room she shared with her mother, and stood irresolute. Her mother would be coming in soon, and would expect to find the potatoes peeled and the table laid. She caught sight of a comic book and, unwillingly, attracted by the garish colors, read one side. "Ah!" she thought in disgust. "Billy!" She thought of her homework. She was so far behind in social studies that she could probably never make it up. It was hardly worth trying. Mercantilism. The rise of the merchant class. She would probably fail. And gym, all those cuts in gym. Miss Fisher, her grade adviser, had called her down yesterday and warned her. "Ah!" she said again. Miss Fisher was all right. She had even been encouraging. "I know you can do it," she had said.

She sat down on the bed and opened her looseleaf notebook at random. A page fell out. She was about to jam it back in, when the freshly inked writing caught her eye. Today's English. Some poem about a vase, and youths and maidens. Miss Lowy had brought in some pictures of vases with people on them, dressed in togas or whatever they were, spinning and reading from scrolls. Why did everybody get so excited about the Greeks? It was so long ago. "Wonderful! Wonderful!" Miss Lowy had exclaimed. How could anybody get so stirred up over a poem? She meant it, too. You could tell from her expression.

"Listen, boys and girls. Listen." A lifted arm enjoined them.

Beauty is truth, truth beauty, that is all
Ye know on earth, and all ye need to know.

There it was, copied into her notebook. Caught by something in the lines, she tried to find the poem in her tattered anthology, not bothering about the index, but riffling the pages to and fro. John Keats, at last—"On First Looking into Chapman's Homer." More Greeks. Here it was—"Ode on a Grecian Urn." The poem, all squeezed together in the middle of the page, looked dry and dusty, withered and far away, at the bottom of a dry well. She saw, not so much words, as an uninteresting, meandering pattern. The big THOU at the opening repelled her. She turned the page to find that the poem went on. Recognizing the last lines, she heard them again, falling so roundly, so perfectly, from the lips of Miss Lowy. She turned back to the beginning. Why "Grecian," why

not "Greek"? With an effort, she began to dig the poem out of its con-
stricted print.

"*Thou foster child of silence and slow time,*" its soft susurrus carried her
on. She read the poem through to the end, trying to remember her
teacher's cadences.

"Write about beauty and truth. Write about life," Miss Lowy had said.

She tore a page out of her notebook and opened her pen. Pulling
over a chair, she rested her book on the sooty window sill. She stared
out at the dusk falling sadly, sadly, thickening into darkness over the
coal yards.

A crash of the kitchen door caused a reverberation in the window sill.
The notebook slipped out of her hands.

"Where'd you get that bottle of pop?" she heard her mother's voice,
hard and sounding more Southern than usual.

A high-pitched, wordless sniveling came in reply. "I asked you.
Where'd you get that pop? You better tell me."

"A lady gave me a nickel. A lady came down the street and ask
me—"

"You lying. I know where you got that money. Gambling, that's what
you was doing."

"I was only pitching pennies, Ma. It's only a game, Ma."

"Gambling and stealing and associating with bad friends. I told you
to stay away from them boys. Didn't I? Didn't I?" Her mother's voice
rose. "I'm going to give you a beating you ain't going to forget."

Billy wailed on a long descending note.

Jeanie could hear each impact of the strap and her mother's heavy
breathing.

"I want you to grow up good, not lying and gambling and stealing,"
her mother gasped, "and I'm going to make you good. You ain't never
going to forget this." When it had been going on forever, it stopped. A
final slap of the strap. "And you ain't going to get any supper either. You
can go now. You can go to bed and reflect on what I told you."

He stumbled past her, whimpering, fists grinding into eyes, and into
the dark little alcove which was his room. Jeanie heard the groan of the
bed as he threw himself on it. She felt a pain in her fingers and saw
them still pressed tightly around the pen.

Her mother appeared in the doorway. She wore her hat and coat.

"Come help me get supper, Jeanie. You should have got things started." Her voice was tired and tremulous, and held no reproach.

"I don't want any supper, Ma."

Her mother came in and sat down heavily on the bed, taking off her hat, and letting her coat fall open.

"I had a hard day. I worked hard every minute," she said. "I brought you something extra nice for dessert. I stood in line to get some of them tarts from Sutter's."

Jeanie rose and silently put her mother's hat on the shelf. She held out her hand for her mother's coat, and hung it up.

Together they opened the paper bags on the kitchen table. She set the water to boil.

As they ate in silence, the three tarts shone like subtle jewels on a plate, at one end of the chipped porcelain table. Her mother looked tired and stern.

"You better fix your brother up a plate," she said, still stern. "Put it on a tray. Here, take this." And she put on the tray the most luscious, the most perfect of the tarts. "Wait." She went heavily over to her swollen black handbag, took out a small clasp purse, opened it, and carefully, seriously, deliberately, picked out a coin, rejected it, and took out another. "Give him this." It was a quarter.

After the dishes were washed, Jeanie brought her books into the kitchen and spread them out under the glaring overhead light. Billy had been asleep, huddled in his clothes. Tears had left dusty streaks on his face.

Her mother sat in the armchair, ripping out the sides of the black dress. Her spectacles made her look strange.

"*Beauty is truth*," Jeanie read in her notebook. Hastily, carelessly, defiantly disregarding margins and doubtful spellings, letting her pen dig into the paper, she began to write: "Last night my brother Billy got a terrible beating. . . ."

Scramble to borrow the social studies homework from a girl in her homeroom, say hello to Barbara, undress for gym, dress again, the torn sleeve, bookkeeping—a blot, get another piece of ledger paper. "This is the third I've given you. You might say thank you." Get to English early.

Slip her composition in under the others, sit in the last seat. Don't bother me. I am in a bad mood. Rows and rows of seats. Rows and rows of windows opposite. She could even read the writing on some of the blackboards, but who cared? A boy learned far out of the window before closing it. Other heads turning. Would he fall? No, he was safe. Heads turned back. A poem about a skylark. From where she sat, she could see about a square foot of sky, drained of all color by the looming school walls. Miss Lowy read clearly, standing all alone at the front of the room in her clean white blouse and with her smooth blonde hair.

Miss Lowy, maybe you see skylarks. Me, I'd be glad to see some sky, she thought and nearly uttered it. Around her, students were writing in their notebooks. Miss Lowy was about to speak to her. Better start writing something. Sullen, Mr. MacIver had called her last week. She felt about for her notebook and pen. It had been a mistake to write as she had done about her brother's beating. They would laugh if they knew. Shirley, who was the class secretary, and Saul, with the prominent forehead. No, he would not laugh. He was always writing about space ships and the end of the world. No danger, though, that her story would be read. Only the best manuscripts were read. She remembered keenly the blotched appearance of the paper, the lines crossed out, and the words whose spelling she could never be sure of. Oh, well, she didn't care. Only one more period and then the weekend. "Lady Jeanie's too proud to come to our party. Jeanie, what are you waiting for? Jeanie's waiting for a Prince Charming with a red Cadillac to come and take her away." If Barbara asked her again, she would go with her, maybe. There was going to be a party at Norma's Saturday night, with Cokes and sandwiches and records and dancing, everybody chipping in. "Jeanie, I need a nickel. Mama, I need a dollar. I need, I need."

The bell rang, and the pens dropped, the books were closed with a clatter. She slipped out ahead of the pushing, jostling boys and girls.

Monday, Miss Lowy had on still another perfect white blouse. She stood facing the class, holding a sheaf of papers in her hand. Most of the students looked at her expectantly. Marion, who nearly always got ninety, whispered to her neighbor. Michael, who had but recently come from Greece—ah, but that was a different Greece—grumbled and shifted in his seat. He would have to do his composition over. He always did.

"I spent a very enjoyable time this weekend, reading your work," said Miss Lowy, waiting for the class to smile.

"Seriously, though, many of your pieces were most interesting, even though they were a trifle unconventional about spelling and punctuation." A smile was obviously indicated here too, and the class obeyed. She paused. "Sometimes, however, a piece of writing is so honest and human that you have to forgive the technical weaknesses. Not that they aren't important," she said hastily, "but what the writer has to say is more significant."

The three best students in the class looked confused. It was their pride not to have technical errors.

"When you hear this," Miss Lowy continued, "I think you'll agree with me. I know it brought tears to my eyes." The class looked incredulous.

"It's called 'Evening Comes to 128th Street.'" Her face took on that rapt look.

Jeanie's heart beat painfully. She picked up a pencil, but dropped it, so unsteady were her fingers. Even the back of Shirley's head was listening. Even the classes in the other wing of the building, across the courtyard, seemed fixed, row on row, in an attitude of listening. Miss Lowy read on. It was all there, the coal yards and Fat Mary, the stoop and the tarts from Sutter's, Billy asleep with tears dried on his face, the clasp purse and the quarter.

"'The funny part of it was, when I woke him, Billy wasn't mad. He was glad about the quarter, and ate his supper, dessert and all, but Mama never did eat her tart, so I put it away.'"

A poignancy of remembrance swept over Jeanie, then shame and regret. It was no business of theirs, these strange white people.

No one spoke. The silence was unbearable. Finally, Marion, the incomparable Marion, raised her hand.

"It was so real," she said, "you felt you were right there in that kitchen."

"You didn't know who to feel sorry for," said another student. "You wanted to cry with the mother and you wanted to cry with Billy."

"With the girl, too," said another.

Several heads nodded.

"You see," said Miss Lowy. "It's literature. It's life. It's pain and truth and beauty."

Jeanie's heart beat so, it made a mist come before her eyes. Through the blur she heard Miss Lowy say it was good enough to be sent in to *Scholastic*. It showed talent, it showed promise. She heard her name called and shrank from the eyes turned upon her.

After school, she hurried out and caught the first train that you could catch only if you left immediately and did not stroll or stop the least little bit to talk to someone. She did not want to meet anyone, not even Barbara.

Was that Billy among the kids on the stoop?

"Billy," she called, "Billy."

What would she say to him? Beauty is truth, truth beauty?

"Billy," she called again urgently.

Billy lifted his head, and, seeing who it was, tore himself reluctantly away from his friends, and took a step toward her.

■ ■ ■

Avi (Avi Wortis)

■ (born in 1937) ■

Most people use the full names that they receive from their parents at birth. Avi Wortis, however, goes only by the name Avi—a name that his twin sister gave him when they were about a year old.

Avi grew up in Brooklyn, New York, in a home where reading and writing were important. His great-grandparents were writers, and so was one of his grandmothers and an aunt. From an early age, Avi wanted to be a writer, too, though he was not a particularly good student. He did read, however—from picture books and comic books to science magazines and many kinds of novels. During his childhood, radio serials aimed at children told exciting tales every afternoon, and Avi was an eager listener.

Avi had a learning disability (diagnosed later) that made reading, spelling, and writing very challenging. When Avi failed all his courses as a high school freshman, his parents sent him to a private school. The small classes there emphasized reading and writing; nevertheless, he needed extra tutoring to graduate. His tutor helped him improve at school and also taught him the principles of effective writing. Avi entered his senior year with plans for a writing career.

With Avi's learning problems, the thought of his becoming a professional writer seemed impractical, even foolish, to his family and teachers. They tried to discourage him. Avi rebelled, determined to prove them wrong. In college, he learned the basics of constructing a play from a professor who had very rigid ideas about what made a play. He even had his students fill out charts as they worked. Avi learned how to organize a story for dramatic impact.

After earning a degree in library science, Avi became a librarian in the theater collection of the New York Public Library. He held the job for twenty-five years. In his spare time, he wrote plays and started a novel. It was only when his own children began clamoring for stories, however, that he turned his attention to children's literature.